GW00368165

DRAMATIC WRITING MASTERCLASSES

DRAMATIC WRITING MASTERCLASSES

Key Advice from the Industry Masters

OLA ANIMASHAWUN

STEPHEN JEFFREYS

CAROLINE JESTER

FIN KENNEDY

KATE ROWLAND

PHILIP SHELLEY

NINA STEIGER

STEVE WINTER

JOHN YORKE

EDITED BY
JENNIFER TUCKETT

CONTENTS

INTRODUCTION

BY JENNIFER TUCKETT

Welcome to *Dramatic Writing Masterclasses: Key Advice from the Industry Masters*. I am the Course Leader of the new MA Dramatic Writing course for Drama Centre London at Central Saint Martins.

Drama Centre London is one of the UK's best drama schools, having trained many of the most successful theatre and screen artists in the UK, and Central Saint Martins is one of the world's leading colleges of art and design. The two organisations have recently come together to create the UK's first MA in Dramatic Writing covering writing for theatre, film, television, radio and digital media.

As part of this new MA, we brought together ten industry professionals who have led the way in the training of dramatic writers in the UK. During the course's first year, with these ten 'Masters', we ran The Year of Experimentation to investigate what dramatic writing training can be in the UK – the first time these top industry professionals had ever worked together and pooled their advice.

This book shares the results of this year with you via ten Masterclasses from our Year of Experimentation Festival – the culmination of our first year – and provides access for the first time to the leading industry training.

Our ten Masters[1] are:

- **OLA ANIMASHAWUN**, founder of the Royal Court Theatre's Young Writers Programme

- **STEPHEN JEFFREYS**, Literary Associate at the Royal Court Theatre for eleven years and creator of Masterclasses which have led the way in Playwriting training in the UK

- **CAROLINE JESTER**, who has been Dramaturg at Birmingham Repertory Theatre, co-author of the book *Playwriting Across the Curriculum* and has pioneered collaborative and digital playwriting programmes worldwide

- **FIN KENNEDY**, winner of the first Fringe First award ever awarded to a schools production and co-Artistic Director of Tamasha Theatre Company

---

1   Job titles correct at the time of the Masterclasses

- **KATE ROWLAND**, founder of BBC Writersroom

- **PHILIP SHELLEY**, instigator of the Channel 4 screenwriting course

- **NINA STEIGER**, Associate Director at the Soho Theatre

- **JENNIFER TUCKETT**, Course Leader for Drama Centre London at Central Saint Martins' new MA Dramatic Writing Course, who previously founded the UK's first formally industry-partnered MA in Playwriting and ran industry-partnered projects on training writers for radio drama and digital media with the BBC

- **STEVE WINTER**, Director of the Kevin Spacey Foundation and co-creator of the Old Vic New Voices 24 Hour Plays and TS Eliot US/UK Exchange

- **JOHN YORKE**, creator of the BBC Writers Academy and former Head of Channel 4 Drama and Controller of BBC Drama Production

These ten Masterclasses offer a unique opportunity to learn from those creating and running the best industry training in the UK, whether you are a writer, student, teacher, arts professional or simply interested in dramatic writing.

Many of these schemes receive thousands of applications a year but what these industry professionals teach or think about dramatic writing and why they created these programmes is often not publicly available.

And if it's not publicly available then how do you know what is being taught or thought about if you're not a part of these schemes? And how do you become a part of these schemes if you don't know what is being taught or thought about? It seemed to us this is a potentially vicious cycle that we wanted to address.

Each Masterclass includes an interview, chaired by a student of Central Saint Martins and Drama Centre London's MA Dramatic Writing course, providing further insight into who these Masters are and additional tips. Some also include Q&As with or input from the audience from our Year of Experimentation Festival.

On that note, I'm delighted to hand over to our first Master, Fin Kennedy, and MA Dramatic Writing student Kritika Arya who has worked with Fin on the first Masterclass.

INTERVIEW ONE
FIN KENNEDY

BY KRITIKA ARYA

KRITIKA ARYA: Can you tell us about who you are and what your background in writing is?

FIN KENNEDY: Yes, my name is Fin Kennedy. I'm a playwright and Artistic Director of Tamasha Theatre Company. I started my career professionally when I did the Goldsmiths' MA Playwriting about 12 years ago now. I got a bursary to do that course. I'd worked in the theatre industry before then in office jobs and done a few fringe shows but it was only on a fully subsidised year on the MA that I was able to take the craft seriously. I wrote my first full-length play for that course which was picked up by Soho Theatre and produced in 2003. This was a play called *Protection* about social workers.

I was also their writer in residence that year. In this position, I started to teach playwriting to their 14-to-18-year-old group. This led to a long parallel career, which I'll talk about later on in the Masterclass, of working with young people.

My second play, *How To Disappear Completely And Never Be Found*, was rejected by every theatre in London before winning the John Whiting Award – one of two big playwriting awards the Arts Council used to run. The play ended up at Sheffield Crucible under Sam West and had a successful run in their Studio Theatre before transferring to London. It's had an afterlife. It's become very popular in America and Australia, and it's also one of the UK's most licensed plays for amateur performance. It's done by students and amateur dramatic societies a lot.

Alongside this, I went back to Goldsmiths and taught on their MA Playwriting, from which I'd graduated, for about ten years. I've got a long association with a school in East London – Mulberry School for Girls – where I've been a salaried writer in residence for a long time. I'll talk about Mulberry later as my Masterclass is going to focus on that as a case study.

All of which has recently led to this new job at Tamasha. That's a potted history.

KRITIKA ARYA: Can you tell us more about your dramatic writing teaching and what you do in terms of it?

FIN KENNEDY: I taught on the Goldsmiths' MA for years. I've just quit because Tamasha is a full-time job but I'm bringing it in-house for Tamasha and we'll be starting a writers' group there.

I specialised in two modules at Goldsmiths. The first was "Research & Performance", in particular the process of acquiring the research skills necessary to investigate and write about subjects beyond your own life experience, and how to do so with authenticity and legitimacy. The second module was "Writing for Young People".

It all started, as I've mentioned, at Soho Theatre, working with their fourteen-to-eighteen-year-old group, which was the first time I'd done anything like that and was a baptism of fire. I don't think I was very good! I kind of made it up as I went along but I learnt a lot on the job.

That led to working for a few years as a freelancer for Almeida Projects. The Almeida Theatre in Islington have an active education department. They call it Almeida Projects and they send theatre makers of all kinds, but particularly writers, into schools in Islington Borough to work with young people to develop response pieces to the main-house shows at the Almeida.

I've written a lot for Half Moon Young People's Theatre, who are a national touring company for teenagers. They produced my first two teenage plays and they have an immersive experience where they send writers into schools in their borough, Tower Hamlets, which is how I first came into contact with Mulberry.

More recently, at Tamasha, I'm currently putting plans in place for the writers' group that I'm going to start in-house at Tamasha. There will be craft-based training about different aspects of playwriting but I also want to start to train that group up as artist-producers able to take responsibility for curating, project-managing and particularly fundraising for their own projects.

It's been a bugbear of mine over the last ten to twelve years that the traditional relationship between writers and organisations renders writers essentially passive. We're almost entirely excluded from the infrastructure of theatre-making, which is weird given that everything starts with us. We're where the ideas come from. We decide whose lives are worth putting a frame around.

Outside of the odd residency programme, you don't get writers running theatre companies. You're always freelance. You wait for the phone to ring. You wait somehow to come to a literary manager's attention. When you do get a commission you're told what the play you're writing is or ought to be and sent away to write some drafts on your own. It's disempowering. My experience started with the knockback I got for *How To Disappear* being rejected by every theatre in London, and having to fall back on my own resources and go "Actually, I can't make a living out of play commissions, how else am I going to use my skills?" I think writers' skills are applicable in lots of different contexts, but particularly in a community context. That's something I'm passionate about training other writers up to do.

KRITIKA ARYA: What do you believe writers need to know about working in schools?

FIN KENNEDY: I do a whole module on this. Amanda Stewart Fisher is an academic at Central School of Speech & Drama who writes a lot about community applied drama and she talks about the writer in residence role in the community context as being a temporary, shamanistic role. What she means by that is that it's not about you. When you get a commission from one of the big companies like Soho or the Royal Court, it is about you and your voice and your vision and your name in lights. It's not like that when you go into schools. This is not only because it's less glamorous and there is not the same infrastructure but also because the close-up work that you'll do is very collaborative.

You might have a group of young people for whom you are the workshop leader as well as the writer and gatherer of the material. That involves a channelling kind of process where you're trying to capture their voices, their concerns, their worldviews and spirit and energy. Then you take all the fragmentary material that they'll generate with you in sessions, take it away, give it your professional polish but hand it back to them in a form that they'll recognise.

It's self-effacing in that respect. I enjoy that process and I enjoy taking myself out of myself. I think it's made me a better artist – it's broadened my palate about the kinds of worlds and experiences I can write about with legitimacy. It's about keeping a stake in real life. It's easy when you're a full-time freelance writer to be holed up in your home/office/garret pontificating about how the world works without actually taking an active part in it.

I've not had a 'proper job', in terms of being at the office every day from nine to five, for a long time. I've got one now with Tamasha but before that I hadn't had one for ten years and it's easy to shed a lot of stimulus and experience that way. So I think it's important for writers to use their skills in a very worldly way.

KRITIKA ARYA: Finally, can you briefly talk about what you've been doing with us?

FIN KENNEDY: I've been working with the MA Dramatic Writing course to curate a festival called the In Battalions Festival. In brief, In Battalions was a political campaign that I started, following a random encounter with Culture Minister Ed Vaizey at a Writers' Guild event at the Houses of Parliament where he said to me "Arts Council cuts are having no effect on British theatre".

That led to me going away and attempting to prove him wrong by undertaking a research-led report in which I gathered testimony and facts and figures from the theatre industry about ways in which Arts Council cuts were having an effect, particularly on our capacity to develop new plays and playwrights.

The results were shocking. I put it online as a free download – it's been downloaded about 25,000 times, been covered in all the broadsheets and had questions tabled in parliament.

It was followed up with a second report, called a Delphi Study. This was a consultation process about ways in which culture professionals can work together to protect risk-taking, irrespective of what the government and the funding situation is up to.

The In Battalions Festival is the first time that we'll all come together in a physical space where we can debate some of the innovative ideas in the Delphi Study. We've been working with one of the students on the MA Dramatic Writing course to found an In Battalions crowd map, which is a crisis-mapping resource-sharing platform. We want to see if we can use that technology for the theatre industry to work together and share resources more effectively.

KRITIKA ARYA: Thank you, and over to you for your Masterclass.

MASTERCLASS ONE
WRITING FOR YOUNG PEOPLE AND THE WRITER AS PRODUCER MODEL

BY FIN KENNEDY

I'm going to talk about my history with Mulberry School. I hope this will provide an insight into my work and practice that you can use or adapt for your own work.

Mulberry is a school in Tower Hamlets, East London. It's a state girls' school but, due to its catchment area, it's about 96% Bangladeshi and Muslim students, mostly second or third generation now. Let's face it, this is not a group you hear from particularly often in British society, never mind British theatre. It's been a privilege to be embedded with them as a salaried writer in residence on and off for about ten years now.

I've done a lot of work for them – curriculum support in English and Drama classes but also extracurricular after-school classes teaching playwriting to students. Also after-school classes teaching playwriting to staff, a professional development course which was an experiment at the time but turned out to be very popular.

However, perhaps the most public-facing, highest profile thing that we did was to develop plays for the Edinburgh Fringe Festival. We did this for three years running in 2007, 2008 and 2009, which was the year in which we won a Scotsman Fringe First award. This was the first time a school has ever received one and it put us on the map. It's led to the first playwrights in schools training scheme, Schoolwrights, which I piloted recently in its first full year and which is now becoming Tamasha Theatre Company's flagship education programme. This involves opening Mulberry up as a training base for other writers who want to get education experience.

There is a long history to that whole process. It predates my involvement at Mulberry, which has got a twenty-five-year history of involving artists in the school, predominantly theatre artists.

I first came into contact with them through Half Moon Young People's Theatre, who sent me into Mulberry. When you get a commission from Half Moon they get you to do a separate project – separate to the play that you're writing for them. They sent me into Mulberry to run a self-contained ten-week after-school drama club in which I worked with students developing a new play. It was about Half Moon giving me contact with their target audience in East London. This indirectly informed the play that I was writing for Half Moon.

It was around the time that Mulberry were thinking of applying for what's called 'Specialist Arts Status'. The Specialist Schools and Academies scheme was something that existed under the last Labour government and schools could apply for specialism status in different subject fields – arts, science, sports etc. Mulberry went for arts and media. It was competitive – you weren't guaranteed to get it, but if you did you got an uplift in funding to allow you to employ artists or specialists from that field to work directly with the students. So Mulberry were able to create a two-day-a-week job for me as playwright in residence in a secondary school. I believe this is probably the first time that's happened.

Mulberry are a great school. They're a state comprehensive school, and a very popular girls' school in the heart of the Bangladeshi community in Shadwell in East London. They put creativity at the heart of the curriculum. Although they excel obviously in drama, they teach all subjects and they have a broad-minded approach to the benefits that having regular creative activity in school can bring to all of those subjects. They believe in what in education we call the 'soft outcomes', which are articulacy, self-confidence, stage presence, assertiveness – all the stuff that you need to get by in life, alongside the obvious knowledge-based subjects as well.

The Specialist Schools scheme was scrapped in 2010 under the coalition government but the work at Mulberry continues under different guises. It meant that we had to become more resourceful and imaginative about how we work together. It was around that time that Tamasha were advertising for Associate Artists. I was freelance at the time and I rang them up and said "What do you want these Associate Artists to do?" They said "Suggest something". I thought "Great, an open brief". So I suggested piloting a playwrights in schools training scheme using Tamasha's Developing Artists programme to advertise for writers to come into Mulberry School for a term and train with me. This would essentially be a mini-version of what we did for the Edinburgh Festival.

At that point it was around 2011 and we'd taken three shows to Edinburgh. In 2010 we held our own festival at Southwark Playhouse in London and I wrote a fourth play which we premiered there.

Each year with Edinburgh we'd evolved the project to add on something new. In the first year, 2007, just taking ten girls from East London to Edinburgh was enough. In 2008 we had a stage manager in residence working with us, so we offered shadowing opportunities in stage management and also with the set designer. Then in 2009 we had a film team who made a film, a radio team, catering, and it started to expand to use all kinds of different subjects areas within the school.

2010 was our festival at Southwark Playhouse. As part of this, we took over Southwark Playhouse and had art displays in the foyer, film screenings and all sorts of things going on. Then 2011 came and we thought "what next?", because there was a bit of a question mark over where we could take this. One of my measures of success for what I've started at Mulberry is always how far it has a life beyond my involvement because it's very easy for one key individual to move on and it all fizzles out.

So the playwrights in schools training scheme was an attempt to try and bring a new generation of writers into Mulberry, to spread Mulberry's expertise around the theatre industry, and also to provide them with a pool of writers who they could commission plays from in the way that they commission plays from me, in the event I was ever not available.

We did that in 2011 and we had eight writers. I was swamped with demand – we had sixty applications for eight places through Tamasha's Developing Artists programme, which convinced me of the demand for this. It was expenses only. We did it all on a shoestring back then. Eight writers came into Mulberry, got their own small group of students to work with over about six weeks in weekly sessions, and were tasked with developing a short play, fifteen to twenty minutes each, in response to these sessions. The students then rehearsed those plays and we put them on at a scratch night at Soho Theatre.

It went so well that Tamasha commissioned me to write a feasibility study for what a longer annual rolling programme of playwrights in schools training might look like and cost. I did this, and they then said "Okay, we can put a bit of money into this" – it was about 10% of the cost – and said "but you'll need to fundraise the rest". Which I duly did. I was very ably assisted by an amazing force of nature called Sofie Mason who runs offwestend.com, a listing site for fringe theatres. Sofia is a great fundraiser from private donors. She got me into the house of a hedge fund manager to do what I think of as proper fundraising – not filling in a form but sitting and drinking the guy's wine and talking about your project and at the end of the night he either gets his chequebook out or he doesn't. We must have done something right because he gave us £6,000, which was a great start. We were then able to go to other trusts and foundations and ask them to match it.

The whole thing took about two years to fundraise, cost about £26,000 and has just come to a head. It's spread over the whole school year now, so the autumn term from September to Christmas is a training phase at Mulberry, which is essentially a repeat of the 2011 term long pilot where the writers get full training with me in school. During this training, I pass on all the creative exercises I've developed over the years to generate material with the students, train them up as workshop leaders, do a little bit of teacher training, child protection training and all the things you need to work in a school. They get their own group of students once a week and develop a short play which they deliver just before Christmas.

Then after Christmas they each go out to another school and set up their own residencies with a bit more autonomy, essentially repeating the process with a new group of students and writing another short play in response. So, by Easter, if they all deliver, I then receive up to twelve short plays.

After Easter, all the teachers involved in the scheme get a masterclass with a theatre director. We had the backing of Soho Theatre this year and Steve Marmion, their Artistic Director, did a Saturday masterclass. Then the teachers are asked to rehearse all the plays with student casts in proper productions, with lines learned and a small budget for set, costume and props. Then we put them all on in the various schools' theatres, as a lot of them have their own theatres. Then we put the plays on at Rich Mix arts centre in Shoreditch and then at Soho Theatre on their main stage.

Getting it up on its feet in its first full year was an amazing learning experience for me. It's now called Schoolwrights. The Playwrights in Schools Scheme had the unfortunate acronym of PISS, which was never going to work, so I had to come up with something else, so Schoolwrights it was. There is a lot about it online. I wrote a piece for *The Guardian* about it. The piece was about how a scheme like Schoolwrights is the case made manifest for public investment in the arts. It will never make money. The free market will never come up with this model. It is the case for public subsidy. It generates value in other ways for those young people, for the artist's skills, for the teacher, for professional development, for the representation of groups in society who we hear from too seldom.

I'm active in trying to bring together the campaigning, research and report-based side of my work, such as In Battalions, along with the actual creative projects which are in some ways almost a more compelling argument than the abstract arguments because the value is so obvious.

We've done the first full year's scheme and we're now taking a year out from doing it. This is partly because we need to fundraise for it again and also because I want to properly evaluate this year's scheme. I learned a lot from doing it and would make a few tweaks next time.

However, it has generated a lot of interest from theatres around the country and particularly outside London. We're looking at fundraising to do a linked version in Thurrock, Essex and Bolton in the North West, with links to venues in both areas.

The nice thing about the model of this scheme is it's scalable, depending on how much money you can raise. We did it with eight writers in the pilot, partly because we weren't paying them properly. Then we did it with six writers, who we did pay properly. I think six is a bit too many. If you do the maths, you end up with a lot of plays, five different schools and sixty-seventy kids and the logistics of that are quite difficult to manage. Also, there is more opportunity for things to go wrong – so-and-so has been suspended, so-and-so is on the geography trip. It starts to affect your ability to rehearse them all.

So I'll probably do it with four writers in future, but if you raise only a little bit of money you could conceivably just do it with two. All you need is one school in which they train and another school or two where they do their second phase and then you bring all the plays together with a theatre partner who can present them in the end.

In terms of cost per head it's good value, especially compared to what main stage productions cost, if you break it down with the amount of young people and teachers it reaches. And of course the plays live on. There is a legacy there. I'm looking into digitally publishing all the plays from this year's scheme and the pilot, which is almost twenty fifteen-minute plays.

I think there is a huge demand for and gap in the market for well written short plays, fifteen to twenty minutes long with a beginning, middle and end, with young people's voices at their heart, and large casts, and which can be read from start to finish in a single lesson, with room left over to discuss and analyse them. Every teacher I speak to confirms that they're on the lookout for plays like that and I think us writers are well placed to provide them.

So I'm going to package all those plays up and see if we can sell them for a one-off fee for a digital publication of twenty short plays which can be used in schools. That might start to generate a bit of royalties for the writers, as well as possibly fund future versions of the scheme.

I'm in discussions with digitaltheatre.com about possibly partnering with us on that. They've got a big education wing, Digital Theatre Plus, which has access to 10% of UK schools and growing.

In time I hope that Schoolwrights might become something that multiplies beyond me. Eventually I'd like to use writers who've been through the scheme in the past to project manage future versions of it.

So that's Schoolwrights. It started with a drama teacher wandering up to me in Half Moon Theatre's foyer and asking if I'd like to come and do a workshop. So if that ever happens to you, I recommend saying yes, because you never know where it might end up.

INTERVIEW TWO
NINA STEIGER

BY LIBERTY MARTIN

LIBERTY MARTIN: I'm talking to Nina Steiger who works at Soho Theatre. Could we start by you talking a little bit about what you do?

NINA STEIGER: I work for Soho Theatre as Associate Director. My responsibility is to find new playwrights and new theatre artists, help them develop their ideas and make sure they are paid and supported as they make work for us. I help develop their projects towards production and further life both at our building and beyond. A lot of my work with writers is across their career from the very early stages, helping them carve out their professional identity and place themselves within an industry. Within a short time, they're usually fine and don't need help placing themselves. However, at the very beginning, often when they're writing their first or second play, the processes of development and production can be overwhelming.

At the same time, I work with the needs of our theatre company to ensure we have great content on our stages, an exciting programme put together with plenty of diverse material to choose from, and an active artistic life. I balance this with the needs of artists, which are to be looked after, developed, supported, produced, exposed. I try to be the catalyst between those two sets of needs.

LIBERTY MARTIN: How do you work with actual play texts or performances?

NINA STEIGER: There's a lot of different ways. I read an inordinate amount of scripts from all different sources. I see a great deal of work. I commission a lot of work, usually reading scripts from the very earliest stages. It can be that the first delivery arrives as twenty-five badly structured pages, but it's my role to see the potential for that fresh start to become its full final seventy-page production and to support the processes that will get us there. I like it because it can be like following a train of thought from idea into the published canon.

LIBERTY MARTIN: Do you call yourself a dramaturg?

NINA STEIGER: I do because it means something to students and to writers and it means something to me. It's the person who is usually there helping. I think of it like curling – I'm usually that person out ahead, scrubbing the ice, projecting trajectories and trying to move things around so that they end up where they should by the smoothest and best pathway. To continue the analogy, I try to help the play go where it needs to go in the best, most efficient, most effective, most powerful way.

I consider myself part of a team. Some dramaturgs are guns for hire and they work with a number of different artists and companies. I consider myself very much a member of a team at a producing theatre. That said, I do a lot of private work, freelancing, and consulting. I consider a lot of the consulting I do with brands and businesses also dramaturgy, in the sense that an idea or story is developed for an audience or market.

I have this one really embarrassing story. I was part of a group of twenty-five people on a fellowship and we had guest speakers come in every day who had access to our biographies and so forth so they would get a sense of who everyone was. One day, we had a speaker who was there to speak to us about representing one's self and capturing your core skills and attributes most effectively. He began, "Someone here is from the north, and someone here said they were a dramaturg. I mean, who even knows what that is? It's pretentious language" and I died of embarrassment. As soon as the session was over I ran to my room to check, "Did my bio say dramaturg, and what other pretentious things did it say?" It turned out it wasn't me – it was one of the other dramaturgs in the group who had used the term – but it was a big moment for me about being clear and speaking to broad audiences in terms they understand.

What that suggests is that, as with everything – and you'll hear the way I talk about making work in the Masterclass to come – keep it really simple. This is an important concept particularly for people pursuing academic lives because there's a huge current pushing you towards a lexicon and a jargon that often overcomplicates. I think you sound cleverest and most attractive when you speak simply and plainly. So, I do call myself a dramaturg, but with those kind of caveats and only in certain circles.

LIBERTY MARTIN: You started your career as a playwright. So, why is it that you do what you do? What was the trajectory of that?

NINA STEIGER: I think the first ten to fifteen years of any career are about the balance between trying to find your feet, make money and get as close as you can to what you feel is the heat source in the room. For me, as a writer, I was like, "Oh my god, I like people who make theatre and it's fun to take things from page to the stage", and that was the heat for me as a writer, as well as a way to express my intelligence, problems and creativity. As I carried on, it became more about directing as that heat source felt stronger. It was as though it was the next level of authorship and a different level of control and interpretation. It was one that was creative, exposing and deeply connected to my interests and issues.

Then I started working at a theatre that worked with new writers, and I discovered that what I really loved was not the nuts and bolts of directing. Because from the time a play got cast and the script was locked, I pretty well lost interest, which is not a good thing for a director. Also, by the time the play had opened, I not only had lost interest, I wanted to leave. I actively never wanted to see the thing again or the people involved, and I took that as a sign that I was not meant to be a director. I'm joking of course, but what I mean is that from the time the script was locked, I felt the heat begin to diminish. For me, the magic was around the tussle for story and style and the possibilities in that.

Another sign early on was that I was often told when applying for jobs in theatres "Please don't have aspirations as a writer or director yourself." I very willingly dropped those aspirations to take on some really great jobs working with and for writers, and I didn't significantly regret that compromise.

I feel that writing will always be there for me. I feel that expressing myself verbally and through images and ideas is something I adore. But I think that's what helps me work with writers. I discovered that the greatest heat, for me, is understanding the soul of a play, what it could become, starting from this fragmented pencil written recipe that arrives on pages and is turned into a live event – to me, that is the ultimate excitement. That's how I discovered what I was.

LIBERTY MARTIN: Do you have some examples of times where that's worked well?

NINA STEIGER: There are examples of where my talent-spotting, which is a big part of my job, has worked well. I have seen people soar into successful and secure careers, and quickly.

For example, one of the first writers I worked with at Soho Theatre was Matt Charman who had never written a play and was working as a valet sorting cars out, and he wrote a wonderful play about that. His writing has taken him to the top of the game. That's a sign to me that I put the right person in the path of the right opportunity.

When I think it's the best is when a piece of theatre has gone from a conversation with an artist over a coffee to something that really catches fire and begins to change the culture. One of the pieces I'm most proud of that I've worked on is by Bryony Kimmings, called *Credible Likeable Superstar Role Model*. It's not a traditional play but very much a piece of theatre about the dearth of appropriate role models for young women and girls in our society and the way they're sexualised. It's the least didactic and preachy kind of evening.

That to me was one that went from "This is what I care about the most" to, within a year, it being on and changing the world around it. So, that's a great example for me.

LIBERTY MARTIN: How does that theatre work link to digital media?

NINA STEIGER: A lot of people who I work with in theatre don't know that I'm wild about the convergence of dramatic writing and digital media. It's not something I bring to bear every day in my job, in my work with various theatre companies or with artists. But I think it's the most brilliant marriage. I always start with this question when I do workshops on this area: "How many people have been on the internet today? How many people were on the internet before they left their house to come out? How many people were on the internet before they got out of bed?" Now some people are going to be like, "Isn't that a bad thing?" And, that's not what we're debating, but it is a bad thing obviously.

However, I believe it's also a really cool thing. I then will ask "How many people have one smart device on you right now? Two? Three?" There's usually three or more – I'm talking about your phone, your iPad and your laptop or something like that. Because it's not unusual that ordinary old us are wired up from the minute we wake up in the morning and, ready to go, we're available. To me, that suggests something very interesting about the way there are performance spaces embedded in that – we are getting stories all day long and it's a space that isn't totally owned by artists yet but there's an amazing opportunity there.

Then there's this other side of it, which is, if that's your life, it's also the life of your audience. I feel I want to say "get in there you artists, and populate that really interesting over-inhabited but under-explored space". So one of the things I thought was that, in theatre and in storytelling, we are so amazing at liveness and uniqueness and experience, there is a real opportunity to bring the two together.

That's how my interest started. What I hope my Masterclass exposes is that I've learnt a lot about theatre and storytelling and liveness through exploring what happens when digital media is part of it. I've learned a lot about what digital media can do through trying to apply what I know about theatre to it. That was the purpose that I thought I should bring to the four-week investigation with the students, and what I'm going to talk about in my Masterclass.

LIBERTY MARTIN: Thank you, I will hand over to you for your Masterclass.

MASTERCLASS TWO
WRITING FOR DIGITAL MEDIA

BY NINA STEIGER

I'm going to talk about what I did over four sessions with MA Dramatic Writing students as part of an investigation during The Year of Experimentation at Drama Centre London at Central Saint Martins. I hope it will give you an idea of some of the ideas we touched on, discoveries we made and the model we used. Then I'm going to give you ten 'take-homes'. You'll be able to infer my values and sensibility from the work we did in this experiment. I hope this will give you ideas for your own models and work.

I started the investigation with the students by trying to explore two questions: "What is dramatic writing in the digital space?" and "what is digital media when there's an author present?" I tried to keep things general and theoretical in the first instance, because I knew we were going to have to get specific with case studies, examples and project pitches in due course.

We began by thinking about "what is dramatic writing?" This was an important question and a hot topic for our first session. We argued with and contradicted each other. It was a tough morning because we had to re-evaluate and re-define a lot of terms. The main criteria we outlined were:

1. Technology – what did we mean by technology?

2. Theatricality – what makes something theatrical versus dramatic?

3. Authorship – because the question is very alive in the culture of today about this continuum of authorship to curatorship. In this very participatory culture, everyone is creating content but does that make you the author or does the person who curates all that content become the author?

Finally we looked at:

4. Participation – because a piece of fourth wall drama like *Miss Julie* – "Don't talk to us while we perform this play at you" – is part of live theatre which purports to be all about this interaction between the audience and the stage. But what happens when you really take interaction to the absolute

maximum degree? What is the highest form of participation of your audience and what happens to the author at that point? And how does technology help the audience be more active as participants?

So there were these north, east, west and south points that we were looking at around technology, theatricality, authorship and participation.

I tried to lead us to one very simple definition of dramatic writing which is: Stories and Audiences. Because the thing that distinguishes dramatic writing from any other writing is that there is a story with an audience.

That audience may or may not be real, it may or may not be the masses, it could be one person. It may or may not be live, the story may not be arranged along dramatic structure, the story may not have conflict, but there is a story and an audience. That felt to me like what we should start with as our ground zero of dramatic writing.

Then we said, "Well, what does an audience do?" Because a story is something we see, it's something we feel, etc. We came to the conclusion that what an author does is create an experience, and that became an important triangle: stories, audiences, experiences.

We also made an important distinction that first morning: that the opposite of digital is not live, it's analogue. We don't use the word analogue very comfortably all the time, but it is an important distinction. It was also one we had to make because we were talking about things that were live and that doesn't mean that they're not digital or digitally mediated.

Those were some of the key discoveries we made. We arrived at the end of that very first morning session battered, bruised, stimulated, annoyed, talking about stories that we'd like to tell and platforms that we could use and what experiences that would create.

Finally, the question I wanted to leave everyone with at the end of that first morning session (I try to end every session with a provocation; I think provocations are good because they're annoying) but the provocation was not, "Is this dramatic writing and digital media?" That's a good question but it's not as provocative and useful as, "What would happen if we considered this dramatic writing?"

This question meant that we opened things out to include a huge amount of things that take place in the digital space. We said, "What if we did allow ourselves to consider that dramatic writing? What would that suggest? And what would that mean? And what would that open us up to?"

That's where we got to on the morning of day one. We then had an amazing guest speaker later that day who talked to us about changing patterns of audience attention from straight TV into the more digital space and the impact that this is having on storytelling.

In the afternoon, things started to progress for us as an ensemble because we started looking at case studies, talking about success stories and cautionary tales as we looked and remembered those things: authorship, technology, theatricality and participation.

We used something called 'The Interesting List' which I've compiled over a lot of years. There's probably sixty projects on it. I add to it every day. I try to give them headings and stuff. I'm going to talk you through four or five of them now. The point of this was to decide what draws us to the projects and practitioners we like. Why do we have a gut reaction of "That's cool" or "I effing hate that; if I came across that I'd kick it into the mud"? What leaves us cold and why?

Okay, I'll talk you through these examples. Let me show you what I've got.

The first one I want to talk about has no digital media, a lot of authorship and a lot of participatory-ness. This is an interesting one because the question is: "is it theatrical?" It's something called *I Know Why She Loves the Moon* created by a group called The Stranglers. What to me is theatrical about it is that it was so ephemeral. It was a stencilled adventure on the streets of San Francisco, and there were two paths you could follow: his story and her story. They started at the same street corner, they walked you all around the Mission district and ended at the top of Mission Dolores Park, encouraging you to look out and think about themes like togetherness, romance, isolation, affiliation, intimacy, and reconsider your position in the urban landscape.

I said I don't like talking fancy about an idea so, let's just say, it was a good time, it was a good story and you, as the audience and participant, had total agency. I would say that there is some highbrow thing going on where, by participating, you create a spectacle, because when this project really caught on, you could see who was doing it in the neighbourhood. What's romantic and exquisite about it is that the scuffing of feet in daily life eventually eroded it out of the landscape, so, like all good plays, what it does is live in your memory, and your subconscious and your heart.

This is the kind of voice it embodies: she tells the audience about the dream journals that she's kept since she was twelve, filled with watercolour sketches and the lyrics of subconsciously composed songs, she tells him about the telescope she uses to examine the intricate surface of the moon. Then it tells you which way to walk, you see a little arrow, and then this is the end: he gets a delicious churro, because we're in the most Hispanic area of San Francisco.

We moved on to something called *The Beckoning of Lovely*. This is an extract from the project:

> "It all started in June of 2008 with Amy's two-minute film entitled '17 Things I Made' which she put up on YouTube. At the end of her film, Amy invited her viewers to come join her in making a cool eighteenth thing together: the meeting place, the Bean Sculpture at Millennium Park in Chicago, the date, 08.08.08 at 08.08pm. She had no idea how many people would come, if anyone would come, but if they did, how would they know her? She'd be the one holding the yellow umbrella. This is what happened.
>
> Oh my God.
>
> It turns out many, many people were there. Hundreds of people even. No one knew exactly what they were there for but, with the light fading fast, Amy assembled the growing crowd on the corner. Who was there?"

Digital media is a propagation tool. In this example, Amy reached audiences through a lot of blogging and YouTube channels but The Thing was a live event. There was authorship, but the process was about distributing authorship to the audience, because what they actually make on the night was not authored at all by her but curated by her. There was theatricality, as this was a 100% live event. So that's how we talked about that one. People liked that one because it's cute and touching.

The next piece I want to tell you about is something called *I Love Bees*, which was one of the very first alternate reality games. A variety of different sources lead you to a website. While you're looking about this beekeeper enthusiast website, all this code comes down – this is ten to fourteen years ago – and basically this is an alternate reality game which is almost like a collective live participatory performance with a game mechanic. What you do is solve real world puzzles, codes, clues, treasure-hunts, challenges to gain. You can do them in any way you want to get to the next stage of the game, but the real world and real technology platforms and the internet are your game board, and you seamlessly hop in and out. It is not authored at all and no one can control the outcome.

I think there are still people kind of playing on this, but not much. One of the things that it was looking at – and this is the thing I think is theatrical about it – was a code would be given out at different times (they give number codes and you eventually find out that it is latitude and longitude) and if you went to that point, there was a payphone, and if you went at a particular time, the phone would ring and give you the next clue, and it would tell you how long you had to solve it, and where you had to be to give the answer to get the next one.

About 5,000 people played this incredibly passionately for about two months. As we move further into the internet age and a digitalised culture, one of the things it was looking at was the obsolescence of things like pay phones, and community collectives working together to solve problems. Those seem to be some of the things at stake, and, I hope, demonstrate that you can embed a strong political and social critique and message into something that appears to be a niche game.

We talked about these as pieces of theatre, and another example of one of these is called *World Without Oil*. I'll give you an example of this so you get the meaning:

> "Gas prices jump to over $4 a gallon. There is a very much police state going on in the street now. Well one way or the other, we're all in this together. This is our local farmer's market."

Game play is over six weeks and posits that in thirty-five days the world's oil supplies are going to be completely gone, what can you do? You get points for what you do. People started these grass roots organisations and interventions, many of which live on today, to begin to address the problem creatively. None of that stuff is real. They're playing out a story that they're writing, which I think is really great. So, there's technology, theatricality, authorship, and it's participatory. To me this was a great example of looking at dramatic writing and digital media coming together. This might not be the thing you're going to write, but it's interesting that you can tell stories with high impact and strong political value.

We talked about some projects that had a lot more technology – technology was the spine. One project was called *Fortnight* made by a theatre company called Prototype, which was a two-week exploration in the city of

Bristol into how communities are formed. The whole thing was played mainly with RFID tags, which is the same technology in your Oyster Card. You'd swipe in and out and be sent on beautiful adventures and missions around the city, and your journey was tracked in an interesting way.

Our City, Our Music is an interesting one to me – this is a location based music project that showcases local bands and emerging filmmakers, rooting the material they make, the art they make, in a specific spot. So, for instance, you might be able to get the recorded live song of a band you love that is motion sensitive, so when you walk by the place where they recorded it you can listen to it and hear their thoughts on the song, how they wrote it, how the place that they live inspires them. You reconnect through the music to a place that you live. What this taps into to me is the audience's appetite for the story behind the art.

Bear 71 is a great example of a technology-oriented art project with strong authorship. This is an interactive documentary made by the National Film Board of Canada. Again this was an example of brilliant digital storytelling. I'll let you explore that one in your own time.

Those are a few of the kinds of projects that we looked at as case studies, and suddenly all of the students moved from saying "I'm not in my comfort zone" to "I am in my comfort zone. I know what I like and I know what I don't like". That's my favourite bit when everyone starts talking comfortably about their taste and aesthetic. We left our first day suggesting that the platform/story dichotomy of what stories are told on what platforms might be too reductive, but trying to articulate a taste and develop a useful framework for further discussion and a much more subjective way of talking about this kind of work, which was important and great.

The students then came up with models that they felt would capture the interesting nuances of talking about work like this. One of the students, Charlotte, said that what she thought was interesting here was people engaging with work and creating their own stories. Everyone had different criteria for what would be the interesting things to look at.

I'll share with you some of what they came up with.

So: how digital is it? How participatory? And, how much does it exist in real time? That was one of the student's, Najma's, criterion.

Charlotte had a great definition: authorship of the audience in the moment shapes the work itself, and so you're looking at many unique possibilities as the audience shape the work that can be made. Do they create a lasting text or is it ephemeral? Can you log the audience's reactions? Or is it just something that's projected to them and taken away?

Those are just a couple of examples which I hope demonstrate how everyone started to dig in to what they thought were the important things as you evaluate a project that pulls together digital media and dramatic writing.

We then talked about how partnerships work in this space – for example *I Love Bees* is a project to promote *Halo 2,* a video game, which followed another alternate reality game project created by the same team to promote A.I., the movie directed by Steven Spielberg, and which was one of the first projects to successfully explore using ARG for marketing purposes. There are huge amounts of partnerships that want to be road-tested or launched into the hands of the audience – brands, other creative properties, businesses, technology platforms. A lot of transmedia stories – I'm going to come back to that in a minute – but a lot of transmedia stories usually represent quite a number of stakeholders. That was something we talked about: what would be a great collaboration? What would be your perfect collaborative setup if you were making a story like this?

What the students had to then do was outline their priorities creatively and define a working style that would work for them within the models that they'd already designed for 'how do you know if this is working?' The question I asked them to consider was "what will make your thing a good digital media dramatic writing project now we're starting to bring in other stakeholders and other partners?"

I'm going to tell you two or three of the ideas that people came up with when we started to talk about what would be a unique project you could make in this space.

Najma came up with something called *Stop the Spread*, which would be a digital project that had live events that promoted peace and healing through a community engaged response to cancer diagnosis. Phil suggested a project called *Give a Bum a Home* which was a reality show where homeless people compete to get a home. It uses the internet to launch a competition and voting from a wider audience, which has a dark embedded political message in there. Liberty proposed a project called *The Most Memorable Experience You've Ever Had*, which was a way of using digital media and live experiences to create an exploration of how money can't buy fulfilment of desires. Julie's project was about how could you crowd-source an audience contribution to help a London detective solve a crime and use a game mechanic and performances as well as a crime-solving lab online to pull people into a fun local experience.

Okay, so we're getting somewhere, people are starting to propose projects. The next area we then discussed was how you know if you're doing it well? What are the metrics for success? Is it how much you earn? How many units you move, so how much money you make? Is it reviews? Is it how many people are involved? Or how involved the five people who are involved are?

This is a different space to the models of the traditional theatre. For example, your criteria could be you sell it to Google for £10 million. We talked about Clint Beharry who works for The Harmony Institute, which measures the impact of stories. We agreed that was a very powerful thing you can look at when you're in the digital spaces measuring impact. When you have a live audience you can count the bums on seats. You can count hits in the online space, but there's different ways of measuring impact and we explored that a lot.

The final assignment was to create a project outline. The students were challenged to devise and pitch a project overview, sort of a blueprint for a piece of dramatic writing, that incorporates digital media, being as free as they like with subject matter: fact, fiction, anywhere in between. They had to conceive this project, give us a five-minute pitch with their title, a visual representation of what it would be, a 140-character tag, like a strapline, that would launch the thing on Twitter, and then a synopsis of how it would work. Ultimately focusing on the stories they wanted to tell, the audiences they wanted to reach and the experiences they wanted those audiences to have.

The final thing that everyone talked about that was very important is legacy. What would the legacy of such a project be? I almost never meet playwrights who are thinking about the legacy of their play. Legacy is something that artists have this very unique opportunity to engage with as a concept. That was something I wanted everyone to be thinking about a little bit.

The outcome was absolutely incredible, what can I tell you?

There was one project called *Floating Life,* which mixed digital education and performance to bring old stories and philosophies into this century.

There was something called *Hello*, which was six houses, six stories of the people who live in them, and the unlocking of the different worlds in this one community where people don't know each other.

There was something called *Let's Hang Out* which was internet dating with and for the audience.

There was something called *The Machine Lives*, which was an alternate reality game about a family's involvement in an illegal hack.

There was something called *Little Warriors*, which was a project that allowed kids to discover their inner warrior as they learnt about local history, using digital media to get inside stories they hadn't heard before.

So, hopefully, that gives you a taste of the project and the model we used.

Now, here are the big take-homes from what we did.

As storytellers, our talent is for telling stories and connecting to audiences. Digital media should only be used to enhance this connection or make it more accessible to people. It shouldn't be about making it more dazzling. It's not about making it cooler or getting more money or complicating things or pulling material onto platforms unnecessarily, or forcing half of the story to be consumed on the internet when it would all be better consumed live. I think the students who I work with know that I'm almost always like, "Why would you do that?"

And that is the great question to ask when you're blending dramatic writing and digital media: why would you do that? My feeling is having the confidence to say, "I'm a great storyteller and I understand audiences" entails the responsibility to keep it simple.

Second take-home: an investigation of the digital is an opportunity to reinvest in your live work and to re-emphasise the live. It's a chance to deeply consider the experience of your audience. That is a very useful thing to do, even if you're writing a one-act play for an evening of shorts.

Consider the experience of your audience, and there is no point messing with cross-platform stories if you can't really try and get inside what it feels like to be the participant audience member in that.

Number three: there is a place for your skills in a new marketplace and a chance to reinvest your skills in the current marketplace. I don't know if anyone will leave the experience of the investigation we had and go get a side-line job writing stories for video games. However, I know that there is a massive market for good storytellers in the digital space. That's something we focused on and I thought was interesting to touch on.

Number four, and this picks up on an earlier point, don't waste time on jargon, for instance, cross-platform, distributed narrative, transmedia and multi-portal are all words that are used interchangeably for projects that incorporate dramatic writing and digital media. What we mean by all of these terms is that there's a story and it gets split across different live and digital platforms. I always urge people to keep it simple. It's as simple as that. Don't worry about what word you're using at what time.

Don't worry too much about living up to what that word is. Live up to the promise of your story – that's what it's all about. It's the story you're telling, the audience you want to reach and the experience you're giving them, and anything else that is top down in terms of the concept that you're trying to fulfil will ultimately almost invariably fail, and alienate your audience.

Number five: this is a great opportunity to think about what the important subjects are for today, and I feel thrilled and satisfied that out of this investigation the subjects people touched on were so vital and so alive and important.

There's this great opportunity to look at powerful social issues, because digital media spreads. You can go deep. Naturalistic family drama is not great for projects like this, but for huge slap-about-the-face, god-I-never-thought-about-climate-change-in-that-way, projects, there's great potential to touch on these issues, whereas writing a straight play about climate change is almost invariably going to be polemical and didactic.

Okay, here's one big take-home, this is number seven: the way to talk about subjects like this is the same – you know I said you can touch on big subjects, well, if you do, it's the same note I would give to straight playwrights all the time: focus on the public and the private.

Liberty's idea was the one where it's a family illegal hack. She allowed herself to talk about public issues of privacy, surveillance, internet security and that kind of thing through a very private lens of a mother and daughter relationship. What she was going to do is explore the conflicts and underlying challenges in those big themes, as they played out across various different scales and forced the audience to think about them too, as both public and private issues. That is a great thing and a good play does that. The personal impact of a public issue, or the public outcome of a personal change. That's what a good play does – sort of map the man and the world.

These projects have to be arranged on that same principle. Things that are in our control, things that are out of our control, the ability of action to change the world. All of those things are very dramatic writing and they work really well in this space too.

Why would anyone want to do this? So, the benefits of cross-platform are: interactivity, multiple access points, meaningful audience authorship, the ability to aggregate participants' material beautifully.

You can make all that come together very, very beautifully using cross-platform storytelling. Meaningful nonlinearity – you can join the story anywhere and it's just as good – is a great opportunity. Meaningful representations of stakeholders and partners – the values of people who have helped you make it – can come to life in a really active, artful, beautiful way. The ability to generate massive buzz – that's what digital storytelling can really allow you to tap into.

What kinds of stories that are theatrical and dramatic suit multiplatform approaches? Stories that have a porous fourth wall, meaning the story needs you to get involved: please let me reach out to you and you reach into me. Those stories work really well. What I call tiny bespokes, which are little one-on-one projects and you're like, "Huh", little tiny things that can stick with you and live with you. I consider *The Beckoning of Lovely* and *I Know Why She Loves the Moon* as tiny bespokes. They work best when you're just with yourself living them and experiencing them and revisiting them and loving them. Big real-world stories like *Oil Crisis* or *The Individual's Right to Privacy Within the City*. Those are big real-world stories that live very well across different platforms, and things that are related to education and world change.

Number nine: I want people to be thinking a lot about what's the best piece of theatre they've ever seen and what made it so, because if you can start to get those into three or four things that become your creative value set, you bring them into your other work and this becomes an extremely rich and rewarding place to be.

The last take-home is a reiteration of what I've been saying all along, which is that what we were tasked with in this four-week investigation was the future of storytelling – it's the most interesting thing in the world to me. I love to engage with it. I think that what we always come back to is something as primal and primitive and atavistic and early and basic as we need, but there's something interesting about, when you're looking at the entire future of storytelling and, by extension, the future of audiences and of experiences, thinking about where you sit in that, as a practitioner, an artist, an educator, a student, a consumer. This is a big moment of reflection and, hopefully, part of your education. This is a chance to consider: where do you feel the most heat? What is your great gift? What is your special skill as a storyteller to offer an audience? Where do you sit within the future of storytelling?

INTERVIEW THREE
PHILIP SHELLEY

BY DAN HORRIGAN

DAN HORRIGAN: I'm delighted to welcome our third Master, Philip Shelley. Philip, can you tell us about yourself?

PHILIP SHELLEY: I am a script editor, producer and trainer. The main thing I do is run the Channel 4 screenwriting course, which I've done for the last four years. I've worked in television drama for the last fifteen to twenty years, script editing and producing quite a few shows for ITV and the BBC.

DAN HORRIGAN: Why do you do that?

PHILIP SHELLEY: I do it because I enjoy it. I enjoy drama. I've always watched a huge amount of television. I used to be an actor before I got into writing. Then I started writing and through writing I got into script editing. I found that script editing and working with writers was the area of work that I enjoyed the most. I think working with writers and helping them fulfil their voice and achieve their best work is creatively interesting and fulfilling.

DAN HORRIGAN: What do you believe writers need to know about script editing and writing in general?

PHILIP SHELLEY: This is what I'm going to talk about in my Masterclass. There are so many different areas to writing. I think there's the whole craft side of it but there's also the business side of it, which isn't talked about so much in this environment. I think it's very important.

The business side is something I've learnt a lot from doing the Channel 4 course as we have a huge number of entries and it is very hard to get onto the course. Inevitably, when we choose the twelve writers we choose, we love their scripts. Their scripts are fantastic but some writers do better off the back of the course than other writers.

That's generally not to do with their talent because they're all incredibly talented writers. It's more to do with how they run their careers as a business, how they conduct themselves as a business, how much research they do about work they want to do, how much television they watch and how they get on working with script editors, producers and directors in quite a pressured environment.

DAN HORRIGAN: Could you tell us a little bit about what you did with us on the MA?

PHILIP SHELLEY: In the first year I did four sessions. The main thing I concentrated on was making sure all the students had quite a broad knowledge of how the industry works, how writers get work, how writers are employed and what projects you're likely to be employed on as a new writer.

We looked at the industry from the traditional broadcasting model to how things are changing at a fast pace, with companies like Netflix and Amazon beginning to commission original drama and what that means for writers. Also addressed was the question of whether you actually need a broadcaster any more or whether you can make your own stuff and make a career and money out of that.

I asked all the students to do research into that initially. Then I asked them to develop an idea for a long-running drama series for television. The reason I did that is because it's the hardest thing to do. It's what broadcasters are looking for most. The Holy Grail for broadcasters is to find the next *Downton Abbey* or *Call the Midwife*, that long-running drama series that gets a big audience and identifies that channel as a brand. That was quite a tall order.

By the end of the four sessions, all the students had a very well worked out outline for a long-running drama series. There were some excellent ideas. That was very exciting. I think some of the students didn't realise quite how good their ideas were. I hope they're still working on them.

DAN HORRIGAN: If you could give one piece of advice to a writer, what would be the one thing you'd say?

PHILIP SHELLEY: Probably just "be persistent and be determined". That's two things. You've just got to stick at it really because you only need one person to like your work. If you write a script and it's rejected by fifteen people and one person takes it on, that's all you need. You do get a lot of knock-backs.

That's one of the things on the Channel 4 course we learn about writing. When you're working with a script editor for the first time and you're not used to that, it's hard. We ask a lot of questions that writers don't want to be asked about their work. Some people thrive in that environment and some people find it difficult.

In any production, if you're working on a show that's in production, it's difficult because there are very tight deadlines that you can't miss. The script has to be to a certain quality by a certain time and there's no way round that. It is tough but you need to have sufficient passion for the craft and for writing that you can ride those bumps and enjoy the process. I think the best writers do it because they love writing. It's a question of making sure you enjoy it.

DAN HORRIGAN: Thank you Philip. I'd now like to hand over to your Masterclass.

MASTERCLASS THREE
WRITING FOR SCREEN

BY PHILIP SHELLEY

I'm going to talk a bit about scripts. I spend my life reading scripts. That's mostly what I do. For the Channel 4 screenwriting course this year we had 1,300 entries. In the past, because the entry period has been open longer, we've had up to 3,000 entries.

I don't read them all. I hire readers and they read them. The readers mark the scripts. I read a lot of the ones with the best marks and also quite a few with the lowest marks – if I read the synopsis and think it sounds interesting.

One of the things that's intriguing is that every year on the course I ask the readers to mark the scripts from A to D. Every year on the course we have two or three Ds because a reader has given a script not a particularly good report and I read the synopsis and think, "Wow. That sounds really interesting". I read the script and like it. Then I have a discussion with the reader and we discuss why we didn't agree about it. Then there are other scripts that a reader will mark an A and I'll read it and not be that taken by it. It's a very subjective business.

One of the reasons I do this job and teach screenwriting is because I think there aren't that many forums for new writers to get their voices heard. There used to be the BBC Writers Academy, which was a very good thing but which sadly doesn't exist any more. BBC Writersroom is a fantastic thing, and the BBC do a lot of good shadow schemes. However, there aren't many courses like the Channel 4 course. There's the Red Planet Prize – and after that I struggle to think of new courses.

The thing I like best about the Channel 4 course is that we ask writers to write original scripts and to write something that is distinctive to them. The brief is that they should be stories that could be seen on Channel 4.

That's not an absolute definition of the script. Often if someone comes up with an exciting idea and it's not quite a Channel 4 idea they'll still write that script because, at the end of the day, what those scripts do for writers mainly is act as a calling-card. Quite a few of those scripts have gone into development with companies who have bought scripts that have been developed on the Channel 4 course.

One of the things I think a lot about is why certain stories stand out for me and what appeals to me about certain scripts. Working on the Channel 4 course with writers who I haven't met before they came on the course (well, I've had an interview with them for ten minutes or whatever, but they come on the course, they write a script over six months and we get a chance to work with them), you learn so much about people and about the way they work.

An important part of the business is that scripts get commissioned from people you've met before, generally. If you're sending scripts out blind to people you've never met, the bottom line is your chances of those scripts getting picked up are not good.

There are two very distinct sides to the business. The most important one is writing a good script, and that's the hard thing to do. Once you've done that, you've only just begun, however, because then you need to get to know people and you need to make the right contacts.

I'm going to talk now about the elements that stand out for me in a successful script which I hope will provide an insight into some of what we cover on the Channel 4 course.

First, if a script is good then usually one of the things it has is a big idea. I'll give you a few examples of that.

There was a writer on the course two years ago called Anders Lustgarten who is a political activist. Everything he writes is political. He wrote a script on the course called *I Am The 1%* which was about a guy who worked for a hedge fund. The hedge fund is basically raping the Greek economy. He begins to see the horrors it is doing and starts this Robin Hood campaign of filtering money from this hedge fund back into Greece. That, for me, was an interesting, topical idea.

Another script we had on the course last year was called *Blood Money* and was about companies like Serco, G4S and Capita. These are the huge service companies who were taking over a lot of responsibilities for areas that governments used to run and don't have the same ethical restrictions that the governments supposedly have. The government is outsourcing lots of things like GP out-of-hours duty, legal services, recruitment for the army etc. This writer had written a conspiracy thriller which was based on that. It was a very recognisable genre in that it was a conspiracy thriller. However the basis, the idea behind the script, was interesting and original.

A final example is this year on the Channel 4 course we had a script about a transgender Asian woman who is living in London. She's from a traditional Asian family in Bradford and her father has a heart attack. She has to go home. She hasn't come out to her family so she goes home as the man she used to be and thinks she's only going to be there for three days. Then her father is taken worse and she has to run the shop that he owns. Just as she is beginning to think about going home she falls in love with a man in Bradford. This was a strong idea again – this time about an Asian transgender woman in the middle of a very traditional Asian community in Bradford.

I was working with that writer and I gave him quite a hard time because he came up with a few ideas that I didn't think were that interesting. This was about his fourth idea. He wrote me a two-page outline for that idea. When I read that outline I knew it was going to be a good script.

This leads me on to something else, which is not only how important the idea is but how important your ability to write an outline is. One of the key parts of the business is writing outlines and pitching. Those are important skills you need to develop. Once you've written that spec script that everyone likes, you're in the door and working with people. If you're working in the industry, people want as much evidence as possible that your idea is going to work before they start paying you any money. It just makes business sense. If your idea is good, it's quite easy to write a good outline. Generally if your idea is good, it will come across in the outline as well as in the script.

To conclude my section on ideas, one of the other things I've noticed from reading the mass of scripts for the Channel 4 course is that not enough scripts are predicated on big, exciting ideas. There are a lot of domestic stories, for example stories about students taking too many drugs and getting drunk. They can be great. *Fresh Meat* is excellent. However, if you get too familiar with those ideas, they aren't that interesting.

If you can write an idea that's got real scale then it puts you ahead of the game. I would urge you all to look at what's going on in the world. If you look at a newspaper front page on any given day, there will be several interesting stories that could be the basis for drama. It's not just reading newspapers. It's looking at the world through your individual lens, looking at things that interest you and thinking about what excites you about the world.

There's the cliché that you should 'write what you know'. I think one of the exciting things about writing is finding out about things you don't know, making yourself an authority on subjects that are of interest to you and then writing about them.

For example, I was at Central Saint Martins for the BBC TV Drama Writers Festival recently and Adam Curtis did a talk about how he sees the modern world. He was fascinating. He does a regular blog on the BBC website which I recommend you have a look at because he was full of amazing stories about his very personal take on news events. He comes from a journalistic background, as a lot of good drama writers do. The writer I was telling you about, who wrote the script called *Blood Money* about the big service industries, was a documentary film maker. That background shows through in her writing.

The second element that stands out for me, and the other side of the coin, is the Dramatic Premise. Whereas the big idea is about intellect and ideas, with a dramatic premise I'm talking more about the emotion behind the idea, how visceral and engaging an idea is and how it grips your emotions.

For instance, I'll tell you again about a couple of other scripts on the Channel 4 screenwriting course which stood out for me for this reason.

There was one script called *Autumn* which was about a seventy-year-old woman who lives in a house with two lodgers. One is an elderly lady in her nineties and the other is an autistic guy in his sixties. She lives this very miserable, rather dull existence until one day she has an argument with the ninety-year-old woman lodger who is becoming more and more unreasonable and hard to cope with – and accidentally kills her. This leads her to becoming a serial killer. She ends up killing three more characters over the course of the serial.

It was a brilliant portrayal of middle England, of a seventy-year-old woman who meets a fifty-year-old woman and they become friends. The fifty-year-old woman finds out this seventy-year-old woman's secret. You could identify and engage with the seventy-year-old woman, the emptiness of her life, and why she was driven to murder four people. That was brilliant writing because you empathised with why she killed those people.

Another script was about a Manchester accountant's office. The boss of this accountant's office discovers that there's been child pornography downloaded onto a computer. He calls someone in to investigate who could have done this. There are five suspects. The story is told from the point of view of three different characters in every episode so you see the same events from three different points of view. That was structurally very innovative and interesting.

Again, there was a strong dramatic premise at the heart of that story. The questions that kept you hooked as the audience were: who did this, are they going to be discovered and what are the consequences going to be?

Another example of the successful use of premise is a recent film called *Blue Ruin*. It's a classic revenge movie. The spin on it is that the protagonist of the movie is a bit of a nerd, completely unsuited to his role as vigilante, and has never done a violent deed in his life. That was a great twist on a very familiar premise.

If you're telling a story make sure it's got a strong dramatic premise at the heart of it. Is it about a kidnap? Is it about a brilliant robbery? Is it about the execution of a murder? Is it about a breakout from prison? For me, something that I learnt from reading so many scripts is: even if a script is fantastically well written, a beautiful read and every other element is fine, if there isn't a compelling story at the heart of it it's not exciting.

The third element which stands out for me is to do with *zeitgeist*. This is a question you will find yourself asked a lot when you're writing a script, particularly if you're writing something that's factually based. The question of "Why now?" Why are you telling this story now? What's its relevance for contemporary society? Why is a big BBC, ITV, Channel 4 audience going to watch this? What's going to appeal to them <u>now</u>?

My next element is about character. Of all these points, I could make quite a strong case for arguing that every single one of them is the most important but probably, for me, character is the most important. If you have a well worked-out story, and it's plotted brilliantly, it won't mean a thing if we don't empathise with the central character.

For instance, in the script 'Autumn' I was just telling you about, the seventy-year-old woman is a beautifully drawn character who you empathise with. I was going to say you empathise with her *despite* her flaws but I think we empathise with characters *because* of their flaws. It's the flaws in characters, as a general rule, that make them interesting and make them engaging.

Another script I was working on was called *Cotton Wool*. It was told from the point of view of a sixteen-year-old girl who comes home from school one day and discovers her mother lying in a pool of blood on the kitchen floor and her father sitting in the garden holding a knife. The father has stabbed the mother. She thinks the mother is dead and she's going to be taken into care. She goes on the run.

This story was about her experiences on the run, mainly in the Lake District before she's brought back to London at the end of the episode. That sixteen-year-old was a beautifully drawn character as she was obviously conflicted about what she'd seen (and grieving because she thinks her mother was dead, although in fact she isn't), and horrified at what she's seen from her father who has never committed a violent act in his life before. She's also quite sexually conflicted because she's in a relationship with a female school friend and then she's attracted to a boy whom she meets in the Lake District. Everything in that story happens from her point of view.

I think character is at the heart of good storytelling. That's the thing that stands out in so many of the best scripts on the Channel 4 course.

Another example is *Blood Money,* the script I was talking about earlier about the service industry companies. In this script, the lead character is a woman who is a security guard in a shopping centre in Sheffield. The catalyst for the whole story is that her eighteen-year-old son goes into hospital for his annual check-up for his diabetes and ends up dead. The quest or the journey of the serial is this woman's quest to find out the truth about what happened to her son. In doing so she uncovers a huge truth about the fact that this hospital, which is the flagship hospital for this new service industry company, is doing terrible things. She is a fantastic character.

In addition to character, I think the best stories are about relationships as well. Some of the best, most successful shows on television are predicated on strong, complex relationships between flawed characters.

I worked on the last two *Inspector Morse* films. The strength of that series was the relationship between Morse and Lewis, which was pretty much a 'bromance' or love story. In the last story, when Morse dies, we had to balance telling a conventional detective story with this end of a love story. That's what brought audiences back to it. It was that relationship between Morse and Lewis, who showed no surface emotion to each other whatsoever, but there was a deep subtext of mutual dependency between them. The same is true with Sherlock and Watson.

Another element that can elevate your story is if it's set in an original, distinctive, appealing story world. The sort of thing I'm thinking about is something like *True Detective,* which is set in the Louisiana swamplands in a backwater community. It is beautifully cinematic but setting is such a strong part of the story. The way the story unfolds is intrinsically linked to the setting.

The script about the Asian transgender woman I've just been working on on the Channel 4 course was completely predicated on the Bradford community in which she had grown up and which she returns to, and on how different that was to the life she's now living in London. In other words, Bradford as a setting was key to the story.

Of other programmes that have been on television recently, *Happy Valley* was a fantastic piece of storytelling. One of the important elements of that was where it was set and the irony of the title. One of the things that worked well was all these unspeakably awful things were happening in the bleak but very beautiful setting.

My next element is about telling your story. This is a bigger, more general point. Some people might question whether this is something you can develop or whether this is something you either have or don't have. I would say that this is something you can definitely improve on. Some writers, in my experience, instinctively have a feel for story. Some writers find that more difficult.

It's so much about the craft of writing, how you structure and tell a story and how you unfold a story, when you release information, how you maintain suspense and narrative tension. That's what story is all about. As writers, I think it's important that you study your craft and think about how storytelling works because a lot of the points I've already discussed are part of this. They're inseparable.

Some stories are just well told because the writer, for instance, withholds information in an intelligent, interesting way so that you keep turning the pages because you want to know what happens. That's what story is. It's about engaging the reader or the audience. It's having a hook. It's having set-ups and then paying them off. As I said, it is about instinct but it's also about technique. It's about learning your technique, thinking about technique and how you can improve that technique.

My next element is to do with humour. This is one thing that strikes me about the scripts that I read every year for the Channel 4 course. I generally set aside a month and I spend probably a good ten hours a day sat in front of my computer, reading scripts. One of the things that makes a script stand out is if I laugh at it. I laugh at so few scripts, which may say more about my lack of a sense of humour. I think it says a lot about the script. If a script is funny, it stands out. If you read a script and it's funny, you don't care about a lot of the storytelling principles because it gives you such joy to laugh at a script and to enjoy a script because it's funny.

One of the scripts that was chosen for the Channel 4 course this year was a beautiful rites-of-passage story about two girls who go on a car journey to four different corners of Great Britain to scatter the ashes of the grandmother of one of them. It's about their relationship on the road. One of them is an actor. There's a scene at the beginning of the script in which she has a meeting with her agent, which in itself was not particularly relevant to the story but it was hilarious. From that moment I was hooked into the script. It was a beautiful piece of storytelling as well. Comedy is important. If you can, get a sense of humour into your script. Obviously not all scripts suit gags or humour. However, humour stands out. If a script is funny, it's exceptional.

My next element is presentation. This isn't one of the most interesting things to talk about but it is important. Write with clarity. Write as clearly as you can so that a script is easy to read. I read so many scripts where I get to the end of a page and I don't know what's happened because it's not very well expressed. As a reader, there's nothing more demoralising than that.

This is the relatively easy stuff. If you can't get this right, you're not going to get the rest of it right. Occasionally you get a very badly presented script that is brilliant – but it's very occasional. Generally, if you read a script and it's not well presented, then it's not well written in any other way either.

Once you've written several drafts of a script and you're in that script from a very subjective point of view, at a certain point you need to put that script away for a couple of weeks, then come back to it and try to read it objectively as a reader would read it.

For instance, it's a question of identifying the characters, and describing the characters when you first meet them, because there's nothing harder than if you read a script and there are five characters introduced on page one and the writer has told me nothing about any of the characters. Then all they are is a name. Often it's not until p.33 that you discover that one of them is thirteen and not eighty-three. It's about communicating your story.

My next element is something that is a bit of a bête noire with me, which is cheating in the directions. So if I was working with a director and I gave a director a script, the director would say to me, "Okay, that's very interesting. How do I film that? You can't film that." Make sure your directions are external, describing what we're seeing onscreen. Be wary of describing internal character motivation in the directions. Screenplays are about the action that we see on screen. They're about what happens on screen.

Write visually, write clearly and think about the directions in terms of the action. It won't all be action, obviously sometimes you are describing something. Make sure it's filmable, it's visual, it's economically written and everything in the directions should have meaning for the story.

Finally, this next element is what I touched on earlier and this is the whole other side of the industry, which is that once you've written this brilliant script that doesn't necessarily have all these elements but has a few of them, then you've got to get your script read.

That's a whole other Masterclass. It's such an important part of the business. You learn about the writers on the Channel 4 course when you get to know them and you work with them for six months, and some people are very happy to pitch themselves, because, as writers, you are pitching yourselves as well as your script.

At the end of the Channel 4 course every year we have a drinks evening and we invite as many potential employers as we can to Channel 4. It's a bit of a cattle market. We have twelve writers with their name labels on. They get to meet these employers. It's probably the most valuable part of the Channel 4 course because lots of meetings come out of these introductions.

In many cases the people that you meet at events like that or in your first meeting with a script editor or a producer in a production company are extremely important. Because if you get on with that person and they like your work and they want to work with you, those relationships can work for years and years for you. There are so many examples of writers and producers who have worked together and have gone a huge way in the industry because they're both good and they enjoy working together.

There was a writer on the course two years ago who I remember I had to physically drag out of a corner where she was talking to three other writers from the course and say, "Come and meet some people". I felt quite mean doing it. Now she is the best networker I know. She's just come to learn that a big part of the business is meeting people and working with other people. You've got to enjoy that. You can't suffer through that or else you won't thrive in the industry.

To conclude, don't think you have to tick all of those boxes. You don't, but try and tick as many as you can. Try and think about those elements in your script and think about whether your script fulfils those points I've talked about. Often if you've got three of those elements out of the nine I've talked about, then you've still got a cracking script.

I think the most important thing is you've got to please yourself. If you don't feel a huge sense of pride and excitement in your script, then you can be pretty sure that no one else is going to feel that either. Don't send your script out to people until you feel that you can get behind that script and you think that it fulfils who you are as a writer. Find those potential employers who are going to be excited by your work. You want to work with the people who get you as a writer and as a person and that you enjoy working with.

It's all about finding your identity as a writer. The more work you do, the more you will know your strengths and weaknesses as a writer. It's a question of playing to your strengths.

INTERVIEW FOUR
STEVE WINTER

BY TUYEN DO

TUYEN DO: Could you tell us a little bit about what you do and how you do it?

STEVE WINTER: I'm Steve Winter and I run The Kevin Spacey Foundation. This came about because I worked with Kevin at the Old Vic Theatre where he was Artistic Director and I was the Director of Old Vic New Voices. For the last ten years we've worked together on developing emerging talent, predominantly actors, producers, directors and, of course, writers.

The Kevin Spacey Foundation funds and mentors emerging artists and their projects. We also offer scholarships to those unable to afford an arts education and create bespoke education initiatives that improve aspiration in young people and develop best practice teaching techniques. We also try to demystify the industry and offer advice and support to those starting out as they develop their craft and contacts.

TUYEN DO: Could you talk about what excites you about working with writers in particular?

STEVE WINTER: I think it's exciting to find new writers with new stories and perspectives and then to try to get their work seen in a venue that's receptive to their style. We have an extraordinary network of new writing venues right across the UK all with the will and enthusiasm to get new work on their stages.

One of the joys of the job is to find a rough diamond, an emerging writer or someone that has been around for a long time but just hasn't got their break, and offer them the support and guidance that they may need to move forward.

It's also about trying to find stories that you've not heard before, stories that are interesting, that might change your opinion on a subject matter, that might offer a wonderful night out at the theatre and a great part for an actor to audition for and be in. I think not many things are more exciting than hearing the germ of an idea from a writer, trying to support it and then seeing it come to fruition.

TUYEN DO: We worked with you on verbatim theatre. Could you expand on how verbatim theatre could help new writers as a form of new writing?

STEVE WINTER: I'll begin by providing a bit of context to the project. I began work on this area at the Old Vic Theatre, where verbatim was extremely important to a strand of work that we call Community, and particularly the Old Vic New Voices Community. It was about involving those that might not necessarily have ever had the opportunity to work in a professional capacity in a theatre.

Every year we made a production by and for Londoners. We tried to target every borough in London in some form or another. We tried to find people who wouldn't necessarily know about the Old Vic or might feel theatre wasn't for them and encourage them to work with us and tell us stories about their life.

Verbatim is important because it puts writers in the room with real people and their life stories and so it can be enormously inspiring because the source material is so honest and unfiltered. To then develop those stories into scripts with actors means writers experience a truly collaborative process that is not just about their vision but a myriad of others. Writers who experience verbatim theatre tell me that it takes their writing in a new direction that is more often than not surprising and challenging. Luckily there have been many great pieces of verbatim theatre recently for writers to learn and be inspired by.

We used verbatim a lot in my time at The Old Vic as it was extremely useful when engaging a cross-section of people for our community plays. Our process in that instance was about capturing as much material as we could through the recording of diverse voices. That meant we often had an extraordinary amount of material to play with. Our cast would then be cast from the local community and would be from sixteen years of age right through to seventy-five and very multicultural. They'd work together collaboratively for five to six weeks on evenings and weekends towards the final production which often had their thoughts, ideas and words threaded together, meaning they felt great ownership over the final production.

In a way, verbatim became a distinct part of our work at the Old Vic because it wasn't me saying, "I commission you. I believe in you. I want you to write this," or, "I don't think you're ready for us but go and speak to wherever". It was really about saying, "Let's offer something for everyone".

TUYEN DO: A final question, if you can answer this: are there any dos and don'ts of verbatim theatre?

STEVE WINTER: I think the key is to not just please yourself and don't assume you know someone's story. Listen and be empathetic and non-judgemental and you'll be surprised, and excited, about what you get in return.

MASTERCLASS FOUR
WRITING VERBATIM

BY STEVE WINTER

I thought I'd present this as a Q&A session and, via that, hopefully I will provide an insight into my time with the Old Vic and Old Vic New Voices, my methods of working, and what it's like to work in the industry.

AUDIENCE MEMBER FROM THE YEAR OF EXPERIMENTATION FESTIVAL[1]: How did you come up with your ideas for the verbatim plays at the Old Vic Theatre?

STEVE WINTER: When we developed each verbatim play at the Old Vic Theatre, we'd begin by, as a team, deciding what subject matter might be interesting to a large group of people, who were varied socio-economically, culturally and age wise. We'd then come up with four or five themes inspired by that subject matter. We'd then go out and test those themes. Whichever theme was most interesting was the one that we decided to creatively explore.

Many of our verbatim plays ended up having an opinion or being opinion-forming. However, we tried to offer balance all along the way. Within the theme, there can be all sorts of different situations, character and moments of drama.

A great example was a piece called *Epidemic* which started off as an idea around the 'epidemic' of social media but became about the epidemic of mental health and how best to address that. In our wisdom we thought the musical theatre format would be the best way to go!

That idea wasn't the one that we thought would take us into the community at first. Initially, it was the epidemic of opinion. We all receive a lot of Facebook messages, emails, and tweets. We're told what we think about things without even thinking about it. We went out and looked at that. The word epidemic was the one that people clung on to.

Then we looked at what is epidemic in London. What was epidemic was mental health so the show became about mental health, which is an interesting diversion from what we originally thought. Within that theme,

1   This Masterclass is based on a Q&A session that took place at The Year of Experimentation Festival at Central Saint Martins. The audience in this and other Masterclasses where the audience is mentioned is taken from The Year of Experimentation Festival

there are a lot of different aspects you can explore. The piece was so emotive, beautifully done and real because these were heart-wrenching true stories of experiences in the mental health environment. They were about either a sibling, relative or the interviewee's own experience of being in a hospital and experiencing illness.

I believe it wouldn't have worked if we hadn't had that authentic dialogue, authentic experience and the situations that you can only find yourself in in real life. There is no way our writers would have come up with those situations.

AUDIENCE MEMBER: If you do a verbatim piece, can you take ownership over it and say you wrote it?

STEVE WINTER: You can say you wrote it because you are moulding something. You're respectful to those that have offered their thoughts but ultimately it's your story and your narrative. You're creating the characters. You're driving the action.

AUDIENCE MEMBER: What about developing a show via interviews via email or similar? Is that okay?

STEVE WINTER: I think that's a good idea as long as you set the parameters before you begin and you say, "This is one of the options that you can give us your thoughts via". In the process that we used at the Old Vic, people were writing things in the workshop but they were also writing emails afterwards because they'd been inspired by something that had been talked about in the workshop.

We did get permission from them first before using that but we took wholesale with their permission because it feels, again, authentic.

AUDIENCE MEMBER: How did you choose whom to interview?

STEVE WINTER: We tried not to be too prescriptive and so we went to as many different places as possible. We'd go to Zumba classes, churches, after-school clubs, housing estates or stand on the street next to overflowing bins and talk to kids as they were walking by. We'd find the people that we needed bit by bit.

The first step is to go out into the community and meet as many people as you can. You sound like an idiot most of the time because the people that you're talking to are not interested. However, you never know who *is* going to be interested. We went to meet some tube workers once and hung around Waterloo station. They were brilliant, hilarious and got it immediately. They had the most fascinating perspective on London and the people that come through the city that they see every day.

You can never assume what someone is like. The breadth of education, the breadth of where they'd come from, the different ages and how they interacted with each other was extraordinary whenever we created a play. We had the most wonderful day driving around with taxi drivers. They really got it as well.

The first point of contact was getting to people in their own environment and then, hopefully, they'd feel comfortable about coming with us to a more theatrical environment. We made contact by advertising, using posters and flyers, using local press, and using Twitter, Facebook and email.

We tended to be very careful however about what we put out there because we didn't want to put people off. We'd talk about the broad outline of what we were trying to achieve and then we'd invite people to come and talk. You're not going to get in a group and play name games and things like that to begin with. You're just coming to talk about what you think about something.

Bit by bit, we then drip fed the theatricalness until they felt more comfortable. It's a fascinating way of finding people. It takes a long time. 'Epidemic' took us eighteen months to pull together.

AUDIENCE MEMBER: How did you find the writer?

STEVE WINTER: We'd find the writer either through other work they may have written or recommendation. We also tried to test them out in a workshop situation to see if they found it inspiring. After which we'd talk about the broad ambition for the piece and see if that's something they felt able to deliver. It was important we engaged writers early on because we wanted them to be involved from beginning to end.

AUDIENCE MEMBER: How does the development process work?

STEVE WINTER: Idea, fundraise, workshop, reflect, commission, perform and evaluate.

To describe the process in more detail, we tended to have short, sharp bursts of activity. We'd break activity into three-month chunks. In a three month chunk we'd prepare for two months and then spend a month getting out there, seeing people, responding, keeping in touch, inviting people to see shows, getting them free tickets, whatever it was which would encourage them to stick with us. Then we sifted through all the material. We had to be clever about what we took away and what we kept. Then we'd have a break and then we'd begin again.

Before that, the big chunk of the time was raising the money. It's a tricky balance because at the beginning we'd think it was one thing but the idea or piece can change, so we had to find sponsors that would come with us. That's a good point to bring in the writer because nobody can sell it better than the writer in the right environment.

It's short, sharp bursts of activity. Then, when we'd get to the production stage, the rehearsal and production happened within about eight weeks.

Rehearsals would be three nights a week and all weekend. That's a huge commitment from the actors if you've got a family or you're working full time. We'd have this extraordinary chart about when people were available. It was a military operation.

At the end of rehearsals, we'd have a production week where we'd do the technical rehearsal, dress rehearsal and then put the show on all in one week. All tickets were free. It tended to be five performances depending on what the scale of the show was. It was a big undertaking. We were only able to do it every two years. I think doing it every year would just be too much.

AUDIENCE MEMBER: Have you used the method of verbatim theatre where actors wear head-pieces to listen to the transcripts of the interviewee as they perform?

STEVE WINTER: I haven't done that but I think it's a fascinating process both for the actors and the audience to observe. It throws up its own challenges and requires skilled actors to interpret the piece naturalistically but also technically as there is a lot going on. You need to try to deliver the piece in a truthful way.

It's usual that when actors get given a piece of verbatim as a script they tend to recognise that it is verbatim quite quickly, because there's something about the beats of the piece when they read it out loud and, ultimately, perform it that feels very real. As human beings we're not very articulate. We go off on tangents. We don't necessarily have a thought process that goes from beginning, middle to end. It's fascinating to see that on paper and what you can do with that.

As an actor it's a real skill to get the script across and still to feel like it's authentic because an actor's first usual approach to the script is to get a biro, underline things, circle commas and circle pauses. Actually you've got to say to them, "No, really try and just get into it without putting any of your stuff on it."

For example, whilst doing the workshop with the students during The Year of Experimentation, that was a big challenge for some of the actors. The challenge was to not layer it with anything and just say it out loud in the way that it was written. It is quite an interesting form for an actor because actors are trained to identify key moments in a script, beats, moments of pause and reflection. That really wasn't what the verbatim experiment I did was about. It was about just trying to get it across in the way that it was spoken originally.

AUDIENCE MEMBER: Did the people who you interviewed come and see the verbatim pieces you created at the Old Vic Theatre and, if so, how did they react?

STEVE WINTER: They did come and see the pieces. Some were thrilled and emotional and felt like we have serviced their story. Others were disappointed because they wanted more of their words in the piece. We experienced both, which can be upsetting because you want to service everybody but it's impossible. We have however had whole interviews which we have put into the play and they've been thrilled. They've been shocked at its power and been thrilled that it's being spoken by a fifty-year-old instead of an eighteen-year-old or whatever we might have done with it. Overall most people see it as a moment in time and a reflection of their thoughts there and then.

AUDIENCE MEMBER: Can the scale of verbatim projects vary? And do you mentor smaller companies who are starting out?

STEVE WINTER: Small or large-scale verbatim projects can be equally powerful. I personally have mentored people in the process of capturing the material but less so in the interpretation of that material as I think it important that that is unique to the individual or company leading the project.

AUDIENCE MEMBER: Is it a good idea to do a workshop of your idea?

STEVE WINTER: It's a great starting point and I suspect you know more people than you think who might be able to participate. It's important to take as many notes as possible so that you can reflect afterwards and see what worked and what didn't work.

AUDIENCE MEMBER: What do you think about writing training in general?

STEVE WINTER: Training wise, I think what's being piloted at Drama Centre London is important because it's industry-led, practical and varied. Places like Soho Theatre also really nurture writers. I'd say there are opportunities but it's a crowded market so there isn't enough to service everyone. I'd advise that writers are aware of the industry so as not to miss out on opportunities.

The other thing that I don't know how you solve is that it's such a subjective industry. That's very difficult when you're submitting work. If your work ends up under the person's nose that understands you and understands your tone, they'll help you. If it goes to the wrong person on the wrong day then they won't.

I think that it would be helpful if we were able to somehow identify a model where you could point people in a direction and say, "Look, your particular tone or your particular style will not work with these people. We know what they are after but it would work for these people here". There tends to be a rather scattergun approach from writers.

I understand that. I was an actor myself. It's the same with actors, the same with directors and the same with producers. Everyone thinks they are right for everything. It's not true. The time spent thinking about where your work might be best placed and having a direction of travel is important. It feels boring and it feels as if you're holding yourself back but that methodical approach is worth considering.

There's a huge amount of people who will write to a particular theatre and have no clue what the last season was, when they programme, what sort of actors they work with or what scale they can make work at. Can they cast a show of yours with eighteen people in? Probably not, so why send it? I think sometimes you've got to go back to the source and say, "Look, what do I believe I can do well?" and throw your energy in that direction rather than trying to achieve too much too quickly.

The next question is then how would you know to do this because you don't get to talk to the right people? The Kevin Spacey Foundation is just beginning. We're looking at ways and models of doing things differently.

INTERVIEW FIVE
CAROLINE JESTER

BY PHILIP JONES

PHILIP JONES: I'm pleased to introduce Caroline Jester. She's a leading UK dramaturg, was the Dramaturg at the Birmingham Repertory Theatre for a number of years, is now pioneering international playwriting programmes and has designed an innovative new online playwriting tool. I'm going to start by asking Caroline some questions about dramaturgy because, for me, when I first heard the word, I was like, "God, what does that mean?" So what is dramaturgy all about, Caroline?

CAROLINE JESTER: I think the word dramaturg in the UK can still be strange within theatres. When I was at the Birmingham Repertory Theatre, my title before I became Dramaturg was Literary Manager, and then it shifted to Dramaturg. That created internal debate along the lines of "we can't give you this title, that's from German theatre, nobody understands what's going on here."

However, for me, a dramaturg is somebody who works in a number of different ways, usually with writers, primarily in theatre. It can be about initiating ideas. It can be about working with a writer or writers in shaping a piece of work. It's about the craft of playwriting as well. I'm very interested in what playwriting, as a craft, can also do in different environments and worlds, outside of theatre.

PHILIP JONES: What have you learnt about dramaturgy over the years you've been doing it?

CAROLINE JESTER: Not so long ago, I worked on a multilingual piece with four different theatres across Europe. When I went to one of the theatres, the Dresden State Theatre in Germany, there were about ten dramaturgs. This was roughly the same size theatre as the Birmingham Repertory Theatre but there were ten dramaturgs within the theatre. I wondered "what do they do?" This led me to start questioning what is the role of the dramaturg in the UK and the role of the dramaturg elsewhere? German theatre is better funded than the United Kingdom. However, what I've learnt about dramaturgy and the role of the dramaturg is that you never have the answer. It's about questioning.

5

PHILIP JONES: In what way is it about questioning?

CAROLINE JESTER: Every writer and every creative project you work on is unique. For me, personally, there isn't a one-way-fits-all dramaturgy. Every writer you work with will have their own sensibility. Sometimes they might not yet know what their aesthetic is or they know what it is but they can't articulate it yet. It's about facilitating that clarity of vision that you can see that they have and helping to shape it. It's about remembering that every creative process is unique.

PHILIP JONES: How does it work in practice when you're working with a playwright?

CAROLINE JESTER: This reminds me a little bit of how they used to talk about playwriting in education. When David Edgar set up the first MA in Playwriting in 1989 the teaching of playwriting was still a relatively young concept and people were like, "What happens?" You've got directors training, you've got actors training, but the writers are supposed to just come into the room. I think, in a way, we're the same with dramaturgs now: "what does a dramaturg do?". Well, a dramaturg doesn't always have to work with a writer. A dramaturg can work with a dance company or with a choreographer. They can work with a visual artist.

I've recently worked with a visual artist on finding a narrative for an examination of the role of public art, so it can be about finding the narrative from the themes and the vision that you start out with on a project. It could be about looking at the structure of a scene with a writer. This could be sitting down and you've got your first draft, and maybe something is not quite working, and so then it's about trying to identify what isn't working. It might be looking at craft in a more structured way, by trying to find the objective of that scene or for that character in order to find out what's not working. It can be many different things.

PHILIP JONES: Do you think questioning in terms of the text and what the play is doing is at the heart of it?

CAROLINE JESTER: I think it's about finding the right questions rather than finding the answers. When we stop questioning then we've reached the end (both with art and with life) and what you want with a piece of work, or a piece of art, is that you never stop questioning, whether it's through the creation of it or through your audience.

PHILIP JONES: What do you think is the one piece of work that you've done that stands out as something that really reflected what you were trying to achieve in the play or performance? Also, how did that achievement occur?

CAROLINE JESTER: Through a moment of conflict. That's the one example that comes to mind. The collaborative piece that I worked on with four different writers. A German writer, a UK writer, a Polish writer and a Croatian writer. Four writers from those four countries. Also, we had a director. I was working as a dramaturg on it recently in the rehearsal room. I was working with the Polish director, and there are very different roles in Europe, in terms of the director being the one who makes the decisions, so to put him in a situation where you had four leading writers, as well as a dramaturg, as well as two actors from each different country, was difficult. He was used to making the decisions and it all going into practice. However, with this project, there were so many people's ideas to work with. At that moment, I felt that I was a conduit for people's ideas in order to try and retain the creative vision of the project, which was about a collaboration.

There was one moment in the rehearsal room where it all fell apart. I instigated that, I think, and in retrospect I would act differently, but it was a necessary part of conflict that then made the aesthetic of the piece clearer because we really discussed what was at the heart of the text. From that experience, I've learnt that sometimes creative conflict is essential for the good of the piece.

PHILIP JONES: One final question I'd like to ask is can you explain what you did with us, as students, in The Year of Experimentation?

CAROLINE JESTER: I'm very interested in objects and spaces telling stories at the moment, probably after working with the visual artist. I'm interested in museums and how the objects, in museums, can tell lots of stories. I was going through doing all of this as a freelance artist when I came to work at Drama Centre London at Central Saint Martins. It was King's Cross that was the inspiration for me. The fact that there was all this regeneration. It had been a couple of years since I'd been to King's Cross so it was a big shock to come to this space that had been regenerated. I kept thinking about, "What are the stories that are being hidden? What are the stories that are being built on? Are there stories that people want to hide?"

I'm interested in using collaborative approaches to generate individual ideas or creative work so first of all you explored your ideas and your themes and found stories around King's Cross. Then we, as a group, started by sitting and telling each other the stories. However, you were starting to interrupt each other's stories, and what became evident, through that process, was there was a mixture of times. We had Boudicca, we had an ape, we had a man in a New Age shop. Then we started to develop what the characters, the themes and the ideas were, but we were thinking in terms of making it an audio piece so when people go to King's Cross there can be many different stories that people can pick up and listen to.

Finally, in groups, you wrote a piece collaboratively on the online playwriting tool that I've developed. Through that, what emerged was the question of audience. What sort of stories can you have readily available at King's Cross? Do you want them to be individual narratives? Or is there something that can hold them together? You created the CCTV, which was a really interesting device because it makes it active. What the CCTV was doing, essentially, was responding to all the stories. That, for me, is an experiment in creating a live piece of work. There's audio and there's a live element, with the person experiencing it in the present.

PHILIP JONES: Thank you. I'm going to hand over to you now for your Masterclass.

MASTERCLASS FIVE
WRITING COLLABORATIVELY

BY CAROLINE JESTER

I'm going to take you through a process in order to provide an insight into the techniques I use when developing collaborative work.

One of my key interests for collaborative work came out of an interest in multilingual work. This began in 2009, just before the last general election, when there was a lot of talk about national identity. Over the last five years the amount of discussion has increased. We've got the Scottish referendum, and the growing debate around whether the UK should or shouldn't stay within the European Union.

Language is central to my interest in multi-lingual work. There are over 300 languages spoken in the UK and yet we very rarely hear other languages on our stages. We're starting to in other media, and occasionally on the stage. However, whilst there are international co-productions, where each country usually provides a member of the creative team, there is very rarely a collaboratively multilingual piece.

My interest in this area continued to develop with the piece I was working on with writers from Germany, from Poland, from the UK and from Croatia, "Europa", with four different theatre companies. It was a great experiment, but what the writers seemed to do was write their own bits. We never got to the place where they were actually collaborating, apart from one scene between the UK and Croatian playwright. They used an online tool I developed for a little bit, but they rejected it. That's fine, they can reject it, but I wanted to then explore why they were rejecting it. What I think, on reflection, was that there needs to be a deeper exploration of the role of playwriting, as it isn't necessarily interpreted in the same way in each country.

In the UK, since the 1968 Theatre Act and the abolition of censorship, the role of the playwright has become generally understood. We have the theatre writers union – The Writers' Guild – so there's a professionalisation of the playwright that doesn't exist in all European countries. I'm interested in exploring European aesthetics so I think we should look at these different practices more.

As another example of my practice, I recently worked in Zagreb with ten leading playwrights from Croatia, and we explored the role of playwriting in the country as a character. For example, we looked at how old is playwriting? If it was a character, is it male? Is it female? Does it have to be gender specific? One of the questions that emerged out of that was "do we include Yugoslavia?" Then we looked at the age of the writers in the group. Nobody was over thirty-five so it became a Croatian and it was a young adult and then, within the theatrical context, that age is not very high up in the hierarchy.

I developed an exercise that I want to share with you now. The exercise is to try and get a sense of whether there are any national responses and differences in national responses. I hope it will provide an insight into my work.

As mentioned, the Europe debate is something that I'm interested in so, in this context, I want to begin by thinking about stories being everywhere. One of the key political stories recently has been David Cameron's reaction to the election for the new Head of the European Commission. I want to share with you a tiny bit from an article:

> '"A bad day for Europe", says isolated and bitter PM, as Commission Chief is elected.
>
> David Cameron took Britain closer to the exit door of the European Union last night following a tumultuous EU summit, at which his fellow leaders inflicted a crushing defeat on the Prime Minister by nominating Jean Claude Juncker for one of the most powerful jobs in Brussels.
>
> In what marked a rift in the UK's long and troubled relationship with the continent, Cameron was left isolated as twenty-six of twenty-eight countries endorsed Juncker as Head of the European Commission for the next five years. "This is a bad day for Europe," said the Prime Minister, as he voiced bitterness over the nomination of Juncker. "This is going to be a long, rough fight. Frankly, you have to be willing to lose a battle in order to win a war. Europe has taken a step backwards with its choice of Commission President".'

What I'd like you to do now is to think about what the actual event of that article is. That's ambiguous in my opinion. It could be David Cameron's vote against the nomination, it could be his public declaration that it's a bad day for Europe. I want you to think about what you think that event is, and try and be as specific as you can.

Write down what you think the event is now before reading on.

Now, let me show you some examples of possible events that came up from The Year of Experimentation Festival:

AUDIENCE MEMBER: Is the event Cameron voting against it? If he hadn't done that, it would have been a thing that happens every four years. The thing that's made it a story is that Cameron has a particular point of view. Cameron has made it an issue. He's the one who's got issues with it.

CAROLINE JESTER: For you, the event is the vote against?

AUDIENCE: Yes.

AUDIENCE: I'd say that the main point, for me, is for David Cameron to ring up and congratulate him on the post afterwards.

CAROLINE JESTER: Well, that's an interesting event as well.

AUDIENCE: I'd like to say him stating the battle lines for the battle ahead.

CAROLINE JESTER: Yes, it's very strong language, isn't it?

AUDIENCE: I was going to say I think what's interesting is maybe the conversations that happened behind those debates. It's something that I know nothing about but it's those back-room politics that go on that seem most of interest.

CAROLINE JESTER: So, for you, an event is a conversation that happened, perhaps immediately after?

AUDIENCE: Yes. I suppose it's that idea of what's the undercurrent all the time.

CAROLINE JESTER: In a way, you're telling us the story there and the theme of how you're interpreting it, not just the event. I've got in my head now a room, something happening, some conversation.

AUDIENCE: I don't really follow politics, so I don't really know the scenario, but I think what I found interesting is he's upset that he didn't get nominated.

CAROLINE JESTER: If you could make that into an event, the event would be his public declaration?

AUDIENCE: A public declaration of being childish. I think it's not really reflected in the article, but it would be the exact moment he finds out. I think that would be the event for everything else.

What I hope I've just started to demonstrate via those examples is that everybody interprets the event differently.

What I'd like you to do now, as stage two of this exercise, is to imagine yourself as a bird. Bear with me. I'm suggesting this exercise because the dawn call of birds is often compared to fifty different languages being spoken. Like the morning news, they're finding out what's happened overnight. They're making everyone aware of their territory. The birds, in this forest, have found a way of understanding each other, without the need for all the vocabulary of their fellow inhabitants. A polyglot Europe could look at this phenomenon to find their own way of amalgamating languages on their continent perhaps. Innovative ways that embrace this diversity, without threatening their loss of cultural heritage.

I want you to now imagine you're in a European forest. I want you to think if you were one of these birds, in a European forest, what sort of bird would you be? It could be a specific bird, or you could just describe the bird. You don't have to be an expert on birds. Think about how old the bird is. How big is it? Does the bird have any specific characteristics? Does it speak any other languages? Does it have any dependents? Imagine your character. You're one of those birds and you're sharing a forest with fifty other birds. Take three minutes to make a note of any thoughts.

I want you to think now about its location. What does its part of the forest look like? What can it see from this part of the forest? Does it get on well with its habitat? Would it like to be somewhere else? Is it up the tree? At the bottom of the tree? Has it been kicked out of the tree? Think about that space. Get the sense of the smell of the space. Location is a very active force in any narrative. Take three minutes to make a note of any thoughts.

What I want you to do now is to think about its objective – it's going to wake up soon, and it's going to be part of this dawn chorus of the European forest. What it's got to do is to have its part to play in telling the rest of the forest what went on in the story we've just read about so I want you to think about its starting point. When it wakes up is it really happy that it's got a new day and it's got to tell people this event? Or is it waking up and feeling despair and doesn't want to share another day in this forest? Take three minutes to make a note of any thoughts.

What we've started to do here is we've looked at where stories come from. Stories are everywhere. We've all interpreted the story in a different way, and we're all starting to think about the event as a starting point. We're starting to think about character. We're starting to think about character and its objective. We're also thinking about location as an active force in the narrative. We're starting now to think about how it's going to tell its event by having its objective as its starting point.

What happened in Croatia, when we did this with a similar exercise using the online playwriting tool, was that some really beautiful scenes emerged. They said this became a history of Croatia. It had a love story and it had a war.

What I'd like you to do now is to spend five minutes writing down your story, whether it's a monologue, a duologue or there are fifty birds in your piece. Just a reminder: your bird is telling the story of the event you have chosen to do with David Cameron's vote and it's your interpretation of what that event can be so it may be a very literal interpretation. Even if you don't write down any dramatic writing, just write down how your character is going to get this across.

I should say it can be in any language as well. Any language that means something to you. It doesn't have to be in English.

Take five minutes to do that.

What we would do now, if we were taking this further, is you would have your individual starting points, your individual objectives, and we would start to create a collaborative scene with you each writing lines for your own character. We would start to see what happened, within this forest, and see what emerged. Because you have an objective, you can start the scene. What we would then do is either continue that and discuss what's emerging or start to explore how to develop that into a piece of work, or it could be just a way of starting to get you to collaborate.

What I'd like to conclude with is to talk about the reason to collaborate and why I'm coming from a slightly different angle in terms of collaborative writing and collaborative playwriting. This comes from a producer and from a practitioner's perspective. I'm interested in challenging the single author perspective. I'm interested in exploring the many diverse forms of storytelling that are all around us. I'm interested in looking at how we can work together and find new dramaturgies. I'm not, in any way, trying to replace anything. I feel that there are lots of different ways of telling stories so we should embrace different ways of storytelling, as well as the individual authored piece of work. The new online playwriting tool I've developed allows you to do this online, so you can each play your own character online and write the lines for this character whilst contributing to the same scene. You don't need to be in the same place – you just type your character's lines into the scene, whilst the other characters/authors are online elsewhere and typing their lines as well. It makes you respond to each other.

I'm also interested in what collaborating can do for your creativity. You may hate to collaborate, but I would say, "Give it a go." When you find out what you hate, you understand your aesthetic a little bit more, and when you're working with people you wouldn't normally work with, you'll learn more about yourself. I'm very interested in how creating collaboratively is about enabling you to take more risks, and, when you take more risks, you'll come to another place in your own aesthetic that you might not know. I'm interested in how it can help develop the artist, how it can help develop different pieces of work, but also how you can use playwriting in different areas to help develop the individual.

I hope you will have the chance to collaborate.

INTERVIEW SIX
OLA ANIMASHAWUN

BY JULIE ZHENG

JULIE ZHENG: Could you tell us about yourself and what do you do?

OLA ANIMASHAWUN: I do two things. I'm an Associate Director at the Royal Court Theatre and I also run my own company called Euphoric Ink. I do the same thing for both of those organisations, which is primarily to run writers workshops with a view to inspiring writers to write. Then, once they've done that, I support and encourage them and try to ensure they do it to the best of their ability. That's a long-winded way of saying I'm a bit of a dramaturg on the side.

JULIE ZHENG: What's the philosophy that you conduct in workshops for writers?

OLA ANIMASHAWUN: My philosophy is just get writing, then let's see what we've got and then to take things from there. It's a philosophy which comes from the Royal Court, which regards the writer as the primary artist, within the collaborative art form, which is theatre. So they're at the centre of that entire process and, without them, we have nothing. People like me are a waste of space, as are directors, as are designers etc. That's first and foremost. Obviously, as I said, it's a collaborative art form – everyone has something to give – but it's writer-led, it's writer-driven, so everything I do is to support the writer in their vision.

JULIE ZHENG: What do you think we, as dramatic writers, need to know about the craft of playwriting?

OLA ANIMASHAWUN: I think that you do need to know about Aristotle and that approach to writing and structuring your writing and your form. Then you need to know about all the other writers who have challenged that form or have broken those rules and those conventions.

I think it's important that you know what the rules and conventions are to begin with – if you've got them under your belt, up your sleeve, inside your soul and at the core then you can have a lot of fun as you move away from that and push the form forward. As artists, essentially what you're always trying to do is break new ground, pioneer new ideas and take things in a new direction.

I think I'd even go so far as to say it's essential that you know what those rules and what those conventions are. Someone said recently, "It's 4,000 years of storytelling." That's a long time. There's a reason why it's endured, and I think you can decide that's either because people got lucky – Aristotle got lucky or writers get lucky and tell stories in a particular way that seems to work – or there's a reason why they seem to work. Why they work is to do with who we are as a species, our understanding of narrative and our understanding of form – how we make sense of life and how we make a meaning out of life.

Once you've got that, there's nothing to say that you can't play around with it, and bend it and reshape it, and do fascinating and interesting things with it, and find new forms and new structures. It might take you another 4,000 years to hit on another one way of working that's not Aristotle, but that's alright. That'll be fun trying.

JULIE ZHENG: Are there any recent examples of plays you've seen at the Royal Court or other theatres that you recommend, that are breaking the form?

OLA ANIMASHAWUN: I've got an answer to that, because usually the answer to that is, "No, not really." However, I saw *Love and Information* by Caryl Churchill at the Royal Court. I would say that that challenged the form of theatre, what theatre is, and what theatre can do. Recently the Royal Court also produced *Not I*, *Footfalls* and *Rockaby* by Beckett, and I would say certainly *Not I* pushes that form and challenges that form and that convention as well.

Most things don't. I think even with *Love and Information*, which is made up of fifty-seven very short scenes, those scenes themselves tend to have that beginning, middle, end structure (as we come to know it) and, even if they don't, we can't help but impose that on them anyway. When we watch things, we tend to want to identify with people. We want to think, "Who is this about? What's this about? What's going to happen?"

However, as an overall piece, I think *Love and Information* did challenge what a play is.

JULIE ZHENG: I'm just starting my writing career and I think we all want to get paid immediately but it's practically not possible, so, on behalf of emerging writers, I want to ask you what your suggestion for us is? How can we balance our paid job and our writing?

OLA ANIMASHAWUN: It's a universal question: how to do it? Because I'm an artist, but a lot of the time people don't want to pay you for your art.

Therefore, it makes sense to work, and in a job that probably isn't art, but it's a job that pays well. I think the important thing is that you need to know yourself, know how you work and what works best for you within the context of knowing that you have to do another job.

An example would be one writer I know who was a teacher and he knew that, while he was teaching, he wasn't going to be able to write. He could make notes, he could have ideas, he could jot ideas down, he can mull things over, but there's no way he's going to write his play. He also knew, as a teacher (and this was one of the reasons why he was a teacher) that they get quite a lot of holidays. Therefore, he would always commit either the Easter break or the summer break to writing his play. He knew that he only had that time, or a section of that time, in which to do it. That worked for him.

It's important that you know yourself, and understand what works best for you. That can change, of course, as you get older, as your life changes, but I think that's the key. Some people commit to getting up two hours earlier each day. They say, "For this period of time, I'm going to get up two hours earlier than I normally do and that's when I'm going to write. I'm going to do that for three months, and I'm going to have my play written by that time. And then after that, I have to go to work, or I have to get my kids up and get them to school."

It's hard. There's no doubt about that. It's hard enough writing a play, let alone trying to live as well. It's understanding that it's tough, but that everything you do resources and invests in what you want to do, i.e. to be an artist.

The way I see it, it's all connected – it's not a case of, "I'm this now, and then I'm that, and then I'm that". There's only one of you, you are you, so everything you do is related to and feeds into whatever you want to do and whatever you want to create.

JULIE ZHENG: Thank you. One last question. In the first half of the interviews, all the Masters had worked with us on the previous Year of Experimentation, but you are going to work with us on next year's experiment so could you tell us more about what you have planned?

OLA ANIMASHAWUN: I love the idea of experimentation for a start and so I embrace that. What we're going to do is carry on something that I piloted earlier this year, with another group, which I'm calling Open Heart Theatre. It's based on the principles of Open Space, which some of you may be aware of and familiar with. Open Space is a way of convening conferences and, essentially, the number one rule, or at least the one that I like the most and have zoned into the most, is the rule of two feet. The rule of two feet operates on the basis that, if you're not engaged with what's happening, or what is happening isn't engaging you, then walk away. It's fine, it's alright, just walk away – go somewhere else to be engaged or to get involved.

I really like that idea. You're taking responsibility for yourself and for whatever is happening. You're not complaining about it, you're not becoming cynical or whinging. You're just going somewhere else. I like that idea a lot, in terms of theatre, and I would like to apply that rule to theatre a lot. Hence the idea of Open Heart Theatre. If the theatre that you're making isn't engaging you then walk away from it – just go somewhere else, do something else. Similarly, equally, you've got to, as a writer, take responsibility to ensure that it's engaging theatre.

You could argue, "Well, of course, everything I write is for people to engage with, and to be engaged by." You could also argue that audiences always have the opportunity to walk away from theatre – people are always walking out of shows.

Well, I think they're not. I had a prime example of this the other night. I was working with a group – we did a little showcase of readings – and someone had said to me they would have to leave before we finished, because they had something else to go to and they got up and left. We were in a rehearsal room, at the Royal Court, which happens to have a door on it that locks when it closes. You can open it and get out but she didn't know that. She got up, three quarters of the way through our showcase presentation, and – because I was on stage, I could see her – I could see the horror on her face when she thought she was locked in. I thought, "God, I so identify with that feeling." There are times it's hard enough to get up and walk out anyway. Not that I do. I don't do that. I don't know if anybody does that. I bet you don't. Most people probably wait until the interval.

Theatre is unlike TV, also film a little bit, but TV definitely. In TV, you have to hold your audience, you have to have them engaged, or else they're going to go. That's all it takes, just one little pause and they're gone and you're writing a drama for nobody. In theatre we get away with murder, because we lock you in, in the dark. It takes a lot of courage and a lot of self-confidence to go, "I'm not engaged." People fall asleep rather than get up and go. However, you shouldn't be doing that, and your theatre shouldn't be doing that. You've got to engage, so that's what we're going to be doing.

We're going to be trying to devise somewhere where we present plays which you can just walk away from or stop if you're not fully engaged with it.

JULIE ZHENG: Thank you, and over to you for the Masterclass.

6

MASTERCLASS SIX
PLAYWRITING

BY OLA ANIMASHAWUN

Now it's easy to shoot your mouth off about being engaged, isn't it? Suddenly the pressure's on when I have to present a Masterclass. Oh well, let's see if I can keep you engaged with this.

I thought that I'd get you to do a little bit of writing. It's nothing scientific, but it is about something really important, possibly one of the most important things in the world… namely you.

What I'm interested in is passion, and that relates to the whole idea of being engaged and walking away when you're not engaged. Partly the reason you're not engaged, is because there's not enough passion or not enough care involved. So this is a very quick exercise on something which I really care about and which I'm really passionate about.

A long time ago I read a book by a writer called Lajos Egri. Some of you will be familiar with him and his theory of premise: having a premise and needing a premise for your play. I subscribe to that.

When I work with writers, I completely infuriate them all the time. It's not a philosophy, but it is a regularly occurring phenomenon. There is a pattern, let's say.

Essentially, what really infuriates and frustrates writers is because I boiled Lajos Egri's theory down to "What do you want to say with your piece?" I can feel the hatred coming my way already, and people going, "Why? What do you mean? I don't know." I can't help it. I think that's really important.

I started to integrate these negative reactions, thinking, "Why is that such a problem? Why is it so difficult? What do you want to say?" Well, I came up with a theory that it's because we here, in this society, live in a good liberal democracy. It infuriates me, but it's good. We don't kill each other most of the time, and what we are is liberal – particularly the writers I tend to work with, and the environment which I tend to hang out in. I'm sure if I hung out in a different environment, it would be completely different. However, this is the kind of environment I tend to hang out in, and the kind of writers I tend to be working with – most of the time – are pretty liberal. We can see both sides of the argument. We can be quite level-headed and reasonable about most things unless we push ourselves. You don't have to scratch very hard actually to get under the surface, and then we're not quite as liberal as we make out or want to be. It's easier. We might stand a chance of getting on better if we are liberal, but really, deep down, or not very deep down actually, we're not that compromising, and not that liberal. That's great, as far as I'm concerned. That's a good thing. That's the good stuff. That's where I want to know what you really think, and I don't need you to agree with me, just as much as I don't need to agree with you.

It's interesting, and that's what drives things forward. That, for me, is what 'premise' is all about. It's what you want to say, and that's what your plays should be all about.

So how do we get to our premise? I don't know is the answer. I actually don't know, but we try and find out by doing things like this.

The first thing I want you to do, and to write down, is proverbs. Those well-known sayings – a stitch in time and those kinds of things. Can you write down any proverbs that you can think of, right now, about anything whatsoever. Thank you. Take just a minute or two to do that.

Now I'd like to share with you a couple of examples that came up from The Year of Experimentation Festival:

AUDIENCE MEMBER: People in glass houses shouldn't throw stones.

AUDIENCE: Pride before a fall.

AUDIENCE: I don't know if this is a proverb. A wink is as good as a nod to a blind man.

AUDIENCE: You can lead a horse to water but you can't make it drink.

AUDIENCE: Don't cry over spilt milk.

AUDIENCE: Don't judge a book by its cover.

AUDIENCE: A stitch in time saves nine.

AUDIENCE: A picture is worth a thousand words.

AUDIENCE: It's not necessarily a proverb. It's something my dad used to say, which I'd take as a proverb, and which was "you're as good as the next person and better than some". He was Irish.

AUDIENCE: All that glitters is not gold.

AUDIENCE: The last straw that broke the camel's back.

I don't know about anyone else but I'm instantly hearing narrative from these examples. I'm instantly hearing possible ideas of what plays might be about, and what plays might be saying. I love that play about the last straw that broke the camel's back. What would that play be?

The next thing I want you to do is make a list. I love lists. If I had more time, I'd tell you why and I'd probably go on forever.

I want you now to make a list, and keep writing and don't censor anything, and try to not stop writing until five minutes is up. You don't have very long, because we haven't got very long, and you're going to make a few lists.

The first list I want you to make is a list that starts with the words, "I think that". "I think that proverbs are a great way of finding a premise", then do another one, "I think that... whatever." "I think that if I eat after lunch, I always fall asleep." "I think that we should never have sent people to school." You see what it's like in my head. Just make a list. Don't censor it, don't judge it, just go, "I think that," and see how far you can get. You should do this now for five minutes.

After five minutes, make whatever you're writing the last, "I think that" and draw a line under it.

Now, do another list that starts with the words, "I realise that" or "I have come to realise that..."

After five minutes, make whatever you're writing the last, "I realise that" and the next list is, "I worry that..."

After five minutes, make this the last thing that you worry about ever, and then write the last list, "I believe that..."

After five minutes, make this the last, "I believe that," for the time being. Draw a line under all of that.

All of that is for you. Not for anybody else. That's just for you to think about, to digest, to cogitate on, reflect on, and then, hopefully, use, turn into a premise, in some way, at some point in the very near future.

According to Lajos Egri, premise is made up of four things and those four things are all contained in one pithy useful little statement that you can write out and that trips off your tongue at any time. When someone says, "What's your play about?" you can go, "It's about this." Bang. You've got this pithy fantastic little statement, and you can write it out and put it above your desk or wherever it is that you work, or keep it on your laptop, just to remind yourself, "That's what it's about. That's what I'm trying to do."

That pithy useful little statement is made up of four things. It's a statement that implies character. It's a statement that implies action or conflict. It's a statement that implies outcome. As you will have noticed, that's only three things – I will get to the fourth in a minute.

So that's where we're trying to get to – we're trying to get to a statement that, in its essence, implies character, action or conflict, and outcome. Maybe some of those proverbs do exactly that. Maybe that could be your premise – that could be the foundation, the rock, of your play. Maybe it doesn't, and you need something else. Maybe you need something a bit more elongated or a bit more sophisticated to convey those three things.

Premise doesn't need to be over complex. It can be quite simple. Here's an example – see if you can guess the play. You may have heard this before: "The sins of the father will corrupt the children," or "are visited on the children". Any guesses?

Ghosts by Ibsen. If you guessed that, you're correct, well done. We felt character, action and outcome.

Here's one more: "Ruthless and heartless ambition will eventually lead to your own destruction". See if you can guess that before reading on.

That's *Macbeth*, and probably other plays as well. That's the slippery thing about premise – it can apply to more than one play.

So that's the idea – that's what you're looking for. That's what you're trying to find: something that's short, succinct, sweet, but lands its point. That's the three components – they imply character, action and outcome. Its particularly useful to think about outcome – often that's the one that people get tripped up on because, of course, outcome gives you your ending, and that's useful. You then know where you're going, before you've even started – that can be important.

What's the fourth thing? The fourth thing is you – it's your passion, your drive, your need to address this belief. That's the thing that's going to make sure that you actually do write the damned play, as some people refer to them. That you do write the play because you have to. You're compelled to because you're so fervent about it. That's the thing that's going to get you through, because it's hard. It is tough, but that's important.

The next point is the format for a premise, which is that it's made up of three things – you've got something, something leads to something, something. For example "the sins of the father leads to the destruction of the children". Something, something leads to something, something. Or, put another way, though it's exactly the same, there is a situation or a state of being, then there is some kind of active verb, and I'm sure you're all familiar with those – leads to, encourages, conquers, those kinds of words, and this creates a new state of being. Finally there is your belief that this is the case.

The premise is just for you. It doesn't have to appear in your play. No one actually has to say it or anything like that. It's not a log line either, or a piece of marketing copy. It's not what you're going to sell your play on. You're not going to market it in this way. It's just for you to know. It's underpinning. It's the foundation of your play.

Here's another small task for you – see if you can come up with the premise for two plays.

The two plays are, and you'll hopefully know of them, *Romeo and Juliet* and *Othello*. How very western and traditional of me, but we've only got a short time. You can either do it on your own, or with a partner, or you can do it on your own and then show it to someone else. See how you get on, I'm going to give you five minutes, because there are other things I need to say.

Before you start, I'm going to give you some good strong active verbs, which are always useful to have. I always carry them around with me, on my Kindle. You might want to write these down, you might just know them – they are: defies, destroys, conquers, defeats, encourages. I just thought I'd share those with you, there are many more.

Take five minutes now to do this task. Come up with premises for *Romeo and Juliet*, and *Othello* using that format. Go.

Done? Sorted? Have you done it? Shall we just hear a couple that people came up with during the Year of Experimentation Festival:

AUDIENCE MEMBER: Love at first sight can be fatal.

OLA ANIMASHAWUN: I would push that and say, "Love at first sight is fatal". Bang. No doubt.

AUDIENCE: Love defies death.

AUDIENCE: It should be death defies love.

OLA ANIMASHAWUN: Well, which is more dramatic?

AUDIENCE: What about defying your parents leads to death.

OLA ANIMASHAWUN: I like that, yes. "Defying parents leads to death". Are you listening, young people? Are you getting that message?

AUDIENCE: There is no happiness in war.

OLA ANIMASHAWUN: I like it. I would turn that around, to give that clear outcome – if you go to war, you won't be happy or there will be no happiness

AUDIENCE: Young love defies family loyalty, with devastating consequences.

OLA ANIMASHAWUN: That sounds like a log line to me. That's how I'd sell that. You almost have to put the word, "If," because it's controversial. "If you fall in love, before you're twenty, it will have devastating consequences" Do you know what I mean? It's getting down to, "This is what I believe."

As I say, these are the thoughts and ideas of Lajos Egri, not mine. I just like to use them.

Also, there's another writer called Buzz McLaughlin, and he took the idea one stage further, because Egri was writing in the 1950s. What Buzz McLaughlin noticed (which is true of myself as well – I blame the Royal Court for this) is that a lot of the outcomes were always negative, and always ended in death, and that not every play has to end in death, and not every play, obviously, is a tragedy.

What he started to do is ask, "Can you have a premise that is positive? Can you invert it?" Essentially, he broke it down as there being two types of play almost, or two types of underlying premise – one being that the central character is unredeemable really, they don't get to learn their lesson, that's why they die. The audience, as a result of watching that, get to see the lesson.

Whereas, in a more positive premise, the character undergoes some moments of learning, some moments of insight, some moment of realisation, and then, in effect, steps back from the brink. This means there's possibly more hope, for the character themselves and for the audience. If we had more time, that would be the challenge, to come up with more positive premises, but see if they are, in fact, still premises.

What you're not going to do now, but I highly recommend that you do at some point, and certainly at some point in the future when you know what you want to write about, and you may even know what you want to say about it, but just to test that or just to make sure, is: give yourself plenty of time, plenty of space, to do some free writing on whatever that theme, subject, or thing is. Take at least an hour, and just write, write, write, write, write whatever it is that you want to say, or you might want to say, or why you particularly want to explore the theme, the idea, or the event. Just write without stopping, and without censoring, and then put it away. Don't even reread it, just put it away and leave it for at least a day, just as a way of interrogating what it is that you want to say.

That's a way of putting into effect those proverbs and those lists – "I believe that, I worry about that, I think that," whatever – and then you're free-writing on the subject, the theme, or the idea. Hopefully, that will take you some way towards coming up with that pithy, useful statement that really is about what you believe, and really is about what you want to say, and then using that as your foundation for your play.

For me, the idea of the premise is not to be reductive. It's not to close things down. It's actually to open them up. It is also a way of interrogating that you're doing exactly what you're intending to do. That you are actually setting out to do something in the first place, other than to just complete a play, and invite people in to watch it, but we don't really know what it's about, or how I actually want the audience to feel at the end of it or during it or at the start of it.

Thank you.

INTERVIEW SEVEN
KATE ROWLAND

BY LIBERTY MARTIN

LIBERTY MARTIN: Kate, tell us what you do.

KATE ROWLAND: I'm the founder of BBC Writersroom, the BBC's new writing department, amongst other roles. Before that, I was Head of BBC Radio Drama. Probably one of the best examples of my work, and one of the first people I worked with when I was a radio drama producer, is Lee Hall. We did eight radio dramas together, and Lee also does the most incredible theatre work, film work, and television work. I think Lee is a good example of how it is about the talent of the writer not the platform that they work for which I think is crucial.

LIBERTY MARTIN: Lee Hall wrote *Spoonface Steinberg*, didn't he?

KATE ROWLAND: He did, and it's one of the most popular radio dramas of all time. I don't know if you know about *Spoonface Steinberg,* but it's worth talking about it for a second. Lee's first play was called *I Luv You Jimmy Spud*, and that was about a little Geordie lad who wanted to become an angel. Because he started wearing frocks, his dad thought he was gay, but in fact what Jimmy wanted to do was develop wings in order to become an angel to save his mum, who had cancer. It was a beautiful tale, very warm and humane but also full of pain.

It was such a success that we came up with a notion called *God's Country*, where we wanted to do four pieces, all taken from the point of view of kids and their faith. One of those was *Spoonface Steinberg* and the others were *The Sorrows of Sandra Saint* and *The Love Letters of Ragie Patel*.

This is an example of when it's about the boldness of a writer. Lee said, "I want to write a sixty-minute drama about a seven-year-old autistic child – a Jewish girl – dying of cancer. I went, "Oh no." "Can you imagine a monologue without punctuation?" was his other thing – there was no punctuation in the text whatsoever.

The power and force of the language and the power of Spoonface's voice was extraordinary. In the end, bringing that out was dependent on me finding someone who could inhabit Spoonface. However, Lee's understanding of what radio could do and the simplicity of what he did, and yet the scale of the ambition of the storytelling, grabbed people.

It stopped lorry drivers on the road. Doctors stopped surgeries. Within seconds we had hundreds of phone calls and it was repeated three times within three weeks. That was about one seven-year-old speaking to a huge audience of people about life and death. That's amazing when you do it.

LIBERTY MARTIN: In relation to wanting writers to be able to work across different platforms, what's special about radio as a form?

KATE ROWLAND: I think radio gives the writer a huge amount of freedom. Also, for a lot of writers, it's the place they start and they return to because it is mostly where we're looking for authored work in the single play. In terms of budgets, a radio drama budget is £20,000 – £24,000. An hour of television drama can be anything from £400,000 to £1 million, so we're not likely to take risks so much.

In radio, the relationship between the writer and the producer, who is also the director, and the writer and the cast and the final product is incredibly intimate. That is why it is also a good place for writers to understand what they can do and to have to work very quickly.

An afternoon play on Radio Four will have an audience of 500,000 people. Think how long that would take you at the National Theatre – quite a long time. You reach people in the most extraordinary places. Every single individual is listening in a different way. Every single person is imagining your characters and seeing them in their very own way. It's a very powerful thing.

The one thing I'd say about radio is that a lot of the time, when people start off, they think of it as the theatre of airways. I'd say that's not helpful because it's much more filmic than that. It's a very visual medium. The dangerous thing a lot of writers do is they overwrite, because they think the audience can't see and they're all a bit stupid, so we'd better tell them, "I'm putting the kettle on now." We can hear it. It's simple things like that.

LIBERTY MARTIN: You commissioned 'The Wire', which was a really interesting slot on BBC Radio Three to showcase radio drama that pushed the boundaries of drama and narrative, where some very exciting experimental ideas were tried. What was special about that slot and what you chose for it?

KATE ROWLAND: The key thing for me about 'The Wire' radio drama slot was, "is it relevant now?" What is its contemporary relevance? Does it tell us about who we are? We gave a lot of writers like Dennis Kelly, Jack Thorne and debbie tucker green their first opportunities with the BBC. I was looking for people who were pushing the boundaries, not just in terms of content but the way in which they wanted to tell that story.

One example was a piece called *The Startling Truths of Old World Sparrows*. What the writer Fiona Evans wanted to write about was how we treat old people and that actually we wouldn't treat a child in the way we treat old people. She did a lot of verbatim interviews, and, from those verbatim stories with very different old people, she shaped and created a three-hander drama. Then those voices were played by seven-to-ten-year-olds.

When you hear somebody being denied going to the toilet for twelve hours because they're waiting for a carer, and when you hear stories like that put into somebody else's voice, then it shifts your perception. It was so powerful.

Radio allows you to do very different things and I would encourage people to think, "What's the story and why does it matter?" Peter Moffat at the BBC TV Drama Writers' Festival talked about the politics of drama and unless you know why it matters and what it's for then he said, "Think about why you're telling that story." I feel exactly as he does about that.

LIBERTY MARTIN: If there was one thing that you could say to writers in general, what would you say?

KATE ROWLAND: I think we'd all say it: be yourself. It's about the original voice. It's your take on the world or your character's take on the world. Never try and second-guess what you think someone is looking for or what a commissioner is looking for. Don't let concept take over character. It never works.

Issue-driven dramas need to have at their heart somebody that we're going to care about and engage with. It's such a simple thing, but so many people don't have a story. We go, "Here's a character. Oh, and nothing is happening to them." That's what I call 'flatlining' – it's just when it goes, "Zzzzz." Nothing has taken place. I quite enjoyed meeting them and then nothing.

Interestingly, with radio, of all the mediums, it has the fastest switch-off, so within three minutes the audience will decide whether they're going to stay with a piece. If you're in the theatre, you're very unlikely to leave until the interval. You've paid, you've sat down, it's quite difficult to get out.

Television: you can be distracted quite easily. But radio is something where you go, "No, I don't like you. I don't want to spend time with you. I don't believe you. I'm going". And people do. That's something we'll talk about in terms of openings.

LIBERTY MARTIN: Thank you, and I'll hand over now to your Masterclass.

7

MASTERCLASS SEVEN
WRITING FOR RADIO

BY KATE ROWLAND

I'm going to take you through a few key pieces of advice in order to provide an insight into my work and what I feel is important in dramatic writing, particularly writing for radio.

My first piece of advice is an interesting quote from Ashley Pharoah: "Be emotionally bold." It's very easy for people to think about being bold in terms of story or plot, but the radio drama I mentioned earlier, *Spoonface Steinberg,* was about life and death. That was emotionally bold. Putting the audience in the place of listening to a seven-year-old who's going to die is massive. So, think about that.

My next point is about openings. Whatever medium you're working in, it's important to think carefully about your opening. Top tip number one is: hit the ground running. You don't have to tell us the backstory, you don't have to fill us in, we're all intelligent beings. I think sometimes people patronise their audience. Tip two: you need to think about the hook. The hook is not just a story hook, but it is also the character's compelling emotional hook. What is it? What's there?

In terms of the opening, also avoid preamble. So many scripts I read spend too long setting up the point at which we arrive. When you move into a house, you do not have all the technical drawings for the house, the architect's specification, and the engineer's report. That's for you and I don't need to see it. That will help you. Keep that out. I can't stress that enough.

My next piece of advice is to take a risk. Most scripts I'd say could start twenty pages in. Think about that. With radio, it's very easy to switch off, and then you won't get the audience. Even though you'll say, "But it is fantastic, those last ten minutes are incredible," it might be but we're never going to get there. It was quite interesting going from being a theatre director into radio, where I could do all sorts of complex things.

In particular, think about your opening sequence. Sometimes before the titles can be like a film trailer in which you set up certain threads. You don't have to explain anything. It's almost like a teaser. It's both an emotional teaser and a story teaser, as long as your key character is going to hook us. That's crucial. We have to want to know, we have to want to turn that page,

7

we've got to be interested in what's going to happen to that character. Your character has to earn their keep. They have to exist in their own right, not be some form of cliché or a stereotype to serve a story purpose because in the end they might engage us very simply for a moment, but we won't stay with them because we won't care about their narrative.

After openings, my next piece of advice is a really important point for me, which is that I will often read a script and all the characters have the same voice. Make sure you don't do this and that they are individual. They are distinct, different people. Every single one of us in this room will speak differently, will articulate our ideas in different ways, and will have a very personal approach. Think about that character – *that* character. They're specific people. They're not general. The place in which they live is not general either, so watch that.

Radio does not get well served by over-populating. If there are too many characters, we can't follow them. It's a very simple rule. I did a great drama once called *Last Bus Home*, based on a true story of a young fifteen-year-old who was murdered. I think that she'd been called a slag. Her friends were upset because she'd been buried in a pauper's grave. They set out to raise money to put her in a proper grave – fifteen-year-olds, an amazing story, all from Hull.

Can anyone spot the problem? Yes, seven Hull lasses. The writer goes, "Yes, but so-and-so is fat, so-and-so is spotty." That's great but not on radio – that's really, really hard. It was a powerful piece, but one of the things I'd say is, if you write a peer group drama – i.e. four twenty-year-olds, and they're all from the same part of South East London, and they're all girls on a hen night – it's tricky. So, two tips: one, don't over-populate, and, two, think about peer groups, whatever that peer group is.

My final piece of advice on characterisation is that you can also have offstage characters that never speak. In *Spoonface Steinberg* there was the cleaner, her mum, and the doctor. We knew those characters. They never spoke. You can find another way to bring those characters into the drama, without sometimes literally having to have them. They need a real purpose to be there.

My next point is about location. Sometimes people are afraid of this, but I would encourage you to let your characters be rooted in a real place, with a real voice, wherever they are from and whoever they are. Just recently on television, Sally Wainwright's brilliant *Happy Valley* was absolutely set in

Hebden Bridge. The place affects the characters: for example, the television series *The Wire* and Baltimore.

There is a tendency in drama to have these abstract 'somewhere in the Midlands', 'somewhere in the North' locations. We don't live in those places. We live somewhere and your characters belong, so don't be afraid of that.

I think that cultural specificity is important – know where it's set and what space those characters inhabit. It has to be real. I'm not saying it has to be kitchen sink real. It just has to be real to the story so that it all belongs together and it all sits together. You can make your own reality.

Dennis Kelly, when he pitched his Wire radio drama to me, just said, "Kate, the story is told in the time it takes a baby to fall from the top of a tower block." That was so powerful. I could see it and of course time stood still in that tower block and every room we went in, but he knew what was going to happen in that time. Radio allows your imagination and the audience's imagination to take flight and to connect, so be bold with the medium.

My next points are about language. Something that Kroetz, a German playwright, talked about, and I'm also very interested in, is the notion of inarticulacy. This can be as powerful as articulacy. Don't be afraid of thinking your characters don't have to join up.

People don't make speeches, people sometimes don't finish a sentence, people don't know what they're going to say, people get tongue-tied, people say, "Uh, uh." That is very powerful on radio. It works. Let that happen if you've got characters who are like that. Jack Thorne did it brilliantly. So don't be afraid of that.

Silence is something important, whether you call it 'pauses', 'silence' or something else. Words have great power, and great meaning, and great potency, but silence does also. It is quite often forgotten when writers are creating radio.

Georges Braque, the Cubist painter, talked about how it's not the object but the space between the objects that counts, and I do feel that with radio. If you think about yourself and your interaction with a radio drama, think about when nothing is said. Think about if ever the radio stops and goes quiet how powerful that is.

I remember the first time I tried to do a sex scene on radio – it was the worst, like you try and pull down a zip or something and it's just comedy.

When you set it up in the audience's imagination, then it is all happening. The story is still being told. You do not have to be explicit in detail in that way.

Language, strangely, is far more potent on radio than it is on stage, on television or when you read it. It resonates and can upset more, so I would always say to writers to think about the language that you use. The Wire radio drama slot has gone but on The Wire slot we used to have a lot of referrals and pushed the boundaries. Just be aware. Different words upset different people and I think it's because of its intimate nature that people feel it more on radio.

My next points are about description. Prose is the worst – people doing great rafts of speeches or descriptions of the place they can see, what's happening to them, how they're feeling. It is not a novel, it's a drama – lean and mean. Just cut it out. There's a tendency in radio scripts for people to over-colour it, or over tell us things, because they think because we can't see, we don't get it. We do get it. Less is more. Always. So, avoid descriptive or prescriptive – don't fill everything in and don't tell us what to think.

Radio is far more – and people don't realise this – like a screenplay. You can write visual narrative. If I leapt off a stage, ran out of a room, slammed the door, cried or something, I would just write that. That is story. That is something happening to your character. It's as powerful as a whole series of words. Mostly people in radio do not write visual narrative, but you can and you should. Paul Abbott said "Writing is rewriting." Boil it down. Look at it, think, "What can I take out? What's crucial there?"

One of the powerful things about radio – but you have to watch not over-using it – is its ability to be both epic and totally intimate. Radio is me talking to you, one-to-one, but I can also show you a huge world. I recorded a drama in the biggest and most dangerous prison in Brazil called Carandiru. The landscape of that and the character of that prison was huge, it was epic, but then it went down to an intimate, to a single voice.

The microphone is your camera. It can get close up. It can zoom in so you get the inner voice. It can be an inner narrative. It can be an internal monologue. There are lots of different ways to describe it. What I would say to you however is it should not be a lazy way to tell your story, so it should not be a narrator.

If you have a narrator, then what is their attitude? One of the first radio dramas I ever directed was Stephen Fry being Balzac. It was a huge classic serial, but at the heart of it was Balzac, and Balzac had an attitude problem.

That is the key: what are they doing that's distinct? If they're just narrating your story, then you need to go back and rethink. If we're getting inside the character's head, why are you doing it that way?

There's a writer who did a brilliant radio drama, which was based on a personal story about her having HIV. She had three voices operating at the same time – one being the voice of the HIV, two, how she was dealing with it, and three the public perception. Each of those voices had a function.

You can speak directly to the audience. It's very powerful, so again think about why you're doing it. If you are doing a monologue – sometimes people think monologues are easy – they're phenomenally hard, because you have to make sure that the dramatic structure is as strong as any kind of normal drama. Sometimes people find their monologues become a prose document, a story, and it's not a character that is living, and breathing, and inhabiting a very difficult, challenging space. Understand how that's going to work for you.

My next key piece of advice is that sometimes writers don't realise that they are in control of the whole thing. When you write your script, how you use music is down to you because you're setting the tone. Use detail for the world that you create. As in any piece of drama, detail it, and make sure that we go into the world.

Music, particularly on radio, can have such a resonant, powerful form. Lee knew in *Spoonface Steinberg* he wanted to use Maria Callas' voice. He knew which piece, why, and how that was going to intercut with particular moments. Someone says, "I want *My Way*" – do you want the Frank Sinatra one or do you want the punk version? You can't be lazy. It's about specificity. What is it doing and why is it there? How does it impact on the characters? Think about those things.

Also, your visual narrative is your sound narrative, and sound, especially within silence, will convey times moving on, for example via a tiny drip of rain. You know what rain is like on a tent – it evokes things. Don't ignore what you can do in terms of that aspect of the narrative, whatever your world is.

Radio is a place in which the audience brings an enormous amount, because it's all in their imagination. I don't know what your imaginations are like, but I hear something at night – wow. Recently, I heard one of the most awful things – suddenly the piano downstairs started playing and I nearly died. Years ago I probably would have rung the police – I'd never have gone down, but when you have a daughter you have to be the brave person – mother. It was a stranger cat. A neighbour's cat had come in, because I had a cat-flap where any cat could come in, and was walking up and down the piano. In my head what was downstairs – what I had visualised, what I thought I was going to see, who was sat at the piano – you can imagine. That's what radio can do. Don't forget what the audience is going to do. You don't have to colour it in. They are part of it, so bring that to bear.

My next points are to do with subject matter. Strangely, with radio, people don't tend to write genre pieces. They don't tend to create thrillers or sci-fi – it's much more the personal world. If you do, then think clearly about the rules of the world that you've created, like Douglas Adams did or like Dominic Mitchell has done with *In the Flesh* – specific and everything belonging to that one place. He knew every single thing about it.

Interestingly, the Radio Four audience – and it's the same with television – really love factual drama. Obviously there are lots of editorial guidelines and things that you have to be careful about and sensitive of. It is an area that a lot is commissioned in, particularly Radio Four, because the audience likes to be informed and taken on a journey, but you have to know that you've got the right permissions.

An interesting drama I commissioned once was called *The Austrian Tourist,* which was based on the true story of an Austrian tourist who was raped by eight boys on the Regent's Canal and it was a powerful, difficult story. Her husband tried to stop us telling the story. Even though he'd sold his story years before to *The Sun*, he suddenly didn't want this story told because he rejected her. What was extraordinary about it was that she, in the end, fell in love with and married the police inspector who investigated it. Out of the darkness came light and it was a really strong piece. But you have to know why you want to do it. Otherwise, it's not that interesting.

The final piece of advice I would give – and it's something I come across a lot – is: work out what you want to write about, why you want to write about it, who those characters are and interrogate those characters. A lot of the time there's a lack of complexity; it feels as if the characters' wants are very simple, and that doesn't really sustain us as an audience in terms of the ambition of your idea and the meat of your idea.

Jimmy McGovern is brilliant on why it's important to drill down and question yourself. You should know what is it that will take your character over the line. What is the one thing, if push came to shove, that you did to that character that would make them pull out a gun or behave in a way that was abnormal? Do you know where their faith is?

If you look at the structure of *The Sopranos,* which is a brilliant drama, you got to know Tony Soprano as a businessman – the fact was that his business was killing people, but he was a businessman. He was also a family man and he was a man in therapy. Those three things, connected structurally, gave so much story, so much complexity, and so much richness to the drama that David Chase created. It's the three things colliding that bring it together, so look at your own drama and think, "What else can I do?"

In term of the business side, mostly radio dramas are forty-five minutes. It used to be that for the forty-five minute Afternoon Play, 25% of the afternoon play commissions on Radio Four are allocated for first and second-time writers, so there's a huge commitment to new talent. Radio Three drama is a much bigger range of lengths, mostly sixty to ninety minutes, but they will do a mix of stage adaptations – fantastic work that's been on – through from Shakespeare to new work. Then Saturday there'll be dramas, and then there's the fifteen-minute drama running across the week in the morning that's repeated in the evenings. That's five fifteens, and then every so often they have 'Fact to Fiction', which is a weekly topical fifteen-minute drama, so there's a mix of lengths. Mainly, it's the forty-five.

Sometimes people think the Radio Four audience is this group of fuddy-duddies. I think the average age is fifty-three, female. I'm well past that, but we're the rock'n'roll generation. Sex, drugs, and rock'n'roll is that generation, so thinking they're all sat around with their knitting and writing a play to suit that is not the answer. Write what you really passionately believe in and the story you want to tell.

INTERVIEW EIGHT
JOHN YORKE

BY CHARLOTTE O'LEARY

CHARLOTTE O'LEARY: John Yorke, can you tell us a little bit about who you are, your background, and what you do?

JOHN YORKE: It seems like I've been in telly forever. I started at the BBC in radio – first as a sound engineer, then later in drama. I then moved to television and worked as a script editor on *EastEnders*. I then worked as a director very unsuccessfully for a bit, went back to *EastEnders* and ended up as Executive Producer. I did that for two very happy years before going to Channel 4 to become Head of Drama. I spent a few years there before I returned again to the BBC as Head of BBC Drama Production. I've sort of done everything, except ITV, though bizarrely I'm currently developing more shows for them than anyone else.

CHARLOTTE O'LEARY: Can you tell us about what you did for dramatic writing in terms of training, because you've got this fantastic book that we've all read on the course?

JOHN YORKE: I became fascinated in the subject about ten years ago, when I'd been at Channel 4 and I went back to *EastEnders*, and I was worried about the standard of writing on the shows.

The output had increased massively and had gone from two episodes a week to four episodes a week, *Casualty* had gone from sixteen episodes a year to fifty-two episodes a year, and there just weren't enough good writers. New writers were joining, but they were failing and that felt to me very unfair and very wrong and, after a while, I realised it wasn't their fault. It was the system. New writers were being destroyed by the system.

I started doing two things – one was trying to work out a way to protect them, but also in the process that became "can you teach writing and how do you go about it"? Out of that came setting up the BBC Writers Academy.

I became obsessed with how you train writers and how you get writers broadcast-ready, because it's a tough, horrible job. If you'll pardon a gratuitous metaphor it's a bit like training fighter pilots in wartime – it's very easy for them to get shot down. So, my job was: "how do we get you up there safely and keep you there?"

CHARLOTTE O'LEARY: What is the answer to that? How do we not get shot down? How do we become better writers? What mistakes do people make?

JOHN YORKE: That's a day to answer that. People make mistakes all the time while they're learning their craft and the only way they stop making mistakes is by trying, and failing, and trying again.

I looked at one statistic which scared me when I went back to *EastEnders*, and it was something like 87% of all new writers failed and were kicked off after the first draft. That seemed insane.

What I realised was: you can't kick them out straight away. You have to create a system that allows them to practise and fail. And, so, the Writers Academy was born out of the idea that you write an episode of *Doctors*, you write an episode of *EastEnders*, an episode of *Casualty*, an episode of *Holby*, and you're supported all the way through that, and if you can't do it by the time you've got 4½ hours of broadcast experience under your belt, then you've had a pretty good shot at it.

If you have a talent for it, you should be able to get through that process, so really it was providing a safety net. Television largely isn't designed to provide safety nets, it is run on economic models, and the one great thing about the BBC is it's not. It's designed to make the world a better place, which seems like a good reason to run training schemes effectively.

Writers fail all the time because the basic mistakes most writers make are bad exposition – telling not showing. It's all the obvious things and you just keep picking people up until they work it out themselves. I firmly believe that if you give people enough space and time, they'll work out how to write for themselves. You don't need to read books to do it – you just need practice, which I'll talk about in a bit when we move on to the Masterclass.

CHARLOTTE O'LEARY: I think one question probably most new writers have is: how do we get onto *EastEnders*? How do we actually get from writing in our bedrooms to working on a show?

JOHN YORKE: There is no one right answer, but there is a global answer, which is: if you're good, you will be discovered. I really believe that. It may take a while and you may have some unfortunate turns on the way. I think it was Debbie Horsfield who memorably said, "There is no conspiracy to keep good writing off television."

People want good writing. People are desperate for good writers. When they hear a voice that excites them, they jump up and down and go, "Wow, where have you been? Have some money." It's ridiculous. That's what happens and it's exciting. Someone who doesn't see your talent may read you first of all, but if you keep submitting, and if you keep writing, then you will get there in the end.

Certain things are useful. If you have an agent, it will help enormously. There is nothing like using contacts. It sounds silly, but use all the personal leverage you can. If you know someone who knows someone who knows someone on those shows, you talk to them. You do all those things. You have to. You have to get read. You will get your first page read and if the first page is good, they'll read the second page, and if the second page is good, they'll read the third page. That's how it works.

I know from my work now I'm working with a much bigger economic imperative, which is I have to pay the bills for my company, I get excited when someone puts a script in front of me, saying, "You've got to read this." It's a lovely feeling. People do want it. You just have to be persistent, because there are an awful lot of people trying to be writers. "Beaver away," I think is the answer.

CHARLOTTE O'LEARY: My next question was going to be what one piece of advice would you give writers, but is that just to beaver away?

JOHN YORKE: It is. When I first started, Matthew Graham, who went on to much bigger things, was twenty-three years old and he was writing on *EastEnders*. I said, "You're very young," and he said, "I've been doing this forever. I've been writing in my room since I was thirteen years old." That's the secret. You just have to write all the time. You just have to learn from your mistakes.

I do meet writers who go, "Yes, I'm not really doing anything at the moment. I'm waiting for someone to find me," and you go, "Oh, okay." That doesn't work. You have to treat it like a craft and be inspired and be true to yourself. Don't copy, but understand the commercial realities of the world you're living in.

CHARLOTTE O'LEARY: Just one very quick last question. You're one of our Masters and you're working with us next year. What are you going to be doing with us?

JOHN YORKE: More of this. The idea is to take the principles that were originally developed in the Writers Academy and talk about what they are and how they work. Inevitably I talk a lot about dramatic structure, which I am unhealthily obsessed by, and how/why it works. I'll probably just talk a lot about that, because that seems to be the wellspring of everything, I think.

CHARLOTTE O'LEARY: Thank you very much. I'll let you get on with your Masterclass.

MASTERCLASS EIGHT
YOU CAN'T TEACH WRITING

BY JOHN YORKE

What I really want to talk about is about teaching writing, the pros and cons of teaching writing and what the worth of teaching writing is. In other words, reflections on the work I've done over the last ten years.

I have entitled this 'You Can't Teach Writing' because that was the position I started out from when I went into this many years ago. It's something I still feel to be partially true. So, I want to explore a contradiction – why I think teaching it is probably impossible, but at the same time why it's worth doing.

As I'm sure you're all aware, we are awash with books that tell us how to write. You cannot move for books that advise us on the rules of screenwriting and how to get ahead in screenwriting – there's hundreds of them. That's just books – the internet has unleashed a whole tsunami of clickbait. "Be a successful screenwriter in thirty days. Just click here."

It's this sort of nonsense that makes a lot of professional writers incredibly antagonistic towards the "guru" industry. The film director Guillermo del Toro voiced this most passionately of all:

"You have to liberate people from film theory, not give them a corset in which they have to fit their story, their life, their emotions, the way they feel about the world. Our curse is that the film industry is 80% run by the half-informed. You have people who have read Joseph Campbell and Robert McKee, and now they're talking to you about the hero's journey and you want to fucking cut off their dick and stuff it in their mouth."

Now del Toro said this a number of years ago, and may well have revised his opinions since then, but the venom with which he expresses his opinion is fascinating. It's very interesting that particularly in Britain – I think far less so in America – there's an attitude that says the teaching of screenwriting is for hacks. The subtext of that, I think it's probably fair to say, is, "I am an artist and I am above joining-the-dots methods of teaching."

David Hare subscribes to a similar point of view: "Genre has almost destroyed cinema. The audience is bored. It can predict the exhausted UCLA film school formulae – acts, arcs and personal journeys – from the moment they start cranking. It's angry and insulted by being offered so much 'Jung for Beginners', courtesy of Joseph Campbell. All great work is now outside genre".

All great work? Pixar's work alone surely proves that wrong – even *Son of Saul* takes its structure from the same DNA as *King Arthur* and *Raiders of the Lost Ark*. But Hare is not stupid, and I suspect his target is not really genre films but rather the strain of teaching typified by Christopher Vogler, author of *The Writer's Journey* – a tome that proclaims the use of a "Hero's Journey", built around Jungian archetypes of myth.

The antagonism directed at any method of dramatic prescription is perhaps best typified by the godfather of modern arthouse cinema – Charlie Kaufman. Indeed his films seem to contain these very arguments against formulisation:

"So, there's this inherent screenplay structure that everybody seems to be stuck on, this three-act thing. It doesn't really interest me. To me it's kind of like saying, "When you do a painting, you always need to have sky here, the person here, and the ground here." You don't, which is interesting".

What Kaufman appears to be really saying is, "You can't teach this stuff. Smash it up. Do something different. That's where all originality lies. Don't read books that tell you three-act structure is important, because it's a load of nonsense."

Hare, Kaufman, Del Toro are all naturally suspicious – and rightly – of lazy, formulaic work. However, their passion to dismiss it exhibits at best a fear and at worst a certain snobbery against the idea that *Transformers* was 4,000 times more successful than Hare's own *Paris By Night*. And I don't think it's acceptable to dismiss that. You may not want to write *Transformers* – I certainly don't – but any writer and any student should be at the very least intrigued by its success. Because if you're not intrigued – and I don't mean this to sound too aggressive – you're a snob. And snobbery is, I think, one of the greatest enemies of art.

This dismissal of the popular, and certainly the ability to teach it, seems a particularly English attitude. It's one which, I'm delighted to say, is slowly starting to change. However, it's an attitude that's worth taking seriously because it's founded on something important – and I know I'm going to sound like I'm contradicting myself here – as it's founded on an understandable snobbery towards the idea that writing is effortless, and with the aid of one or two books is easy. It's an attitude I feel myself when I look at screenwriting books. When you read things like: "There has to be an inciting incident on p.23 – not p.20, not p.24, p.23. Put it there", it drives me to despair. What font size are you using? It's ridiculous. It's nonsensical – and it's nonsensical for a very simple reason: because it doesn't tell you *why*. And *why* is the most important question of all. "Put it there". WHY? You have to say "WHY?", because what pretty much every screenwriting book lacks is basic empirical rigour. Proof. There is no analysis, there's just "Put it there" – and "put it there" is not enough.

So when a screenwriting guru stands up and lectures you on what, without empirical rigour, can only be described as snake oil, they are not giving you knowledge. At best they are giving you dogma and at worst demagoguery. They are snake oil salesmen. Shamans enchanting you with their spell: "This is the answer. Do it this way. Follow me. Give me money. I will make you rich." As with any medicine, if they can't tell how it works, you really shouldn't be taking it at all.

And of course I talk to you now, and you're bright, smart people so you're almost certainly thinking, "That's all very well, but aren't you doing the same thing?"

Let me see if I can extricate myself from the accusation – let us go back to basic principles.

Arguably, you can't teach writing. You either have the talent to write or you don't. At some level – think of *Amadeus*, think of Mozart, think of the God-given genius of an eight-year-old boy, compared to Salieri, who'd been practising and playing all his life. Weren't we all Salieri? And if so, why try and teach – or learn anything at all?

Rationally there are only two arguments to counter this. The first I touched on earlier when I was talking with Charlotte, which is practice makes perfect. It's the rule of 10,000 hours: if you work consistently and steadily over a huge period of time, you will learn. You must learn. You must get better. That seems to me fundamental.

The second thing you have to do is you have to agree with a premise. It's a premise I think most people now concur with, but which, when I started doing this ten years ago, was greeted far more sceptically. That premise is this – writing does have rules.

The most important thing to remember, as Charlie Kaufman keeps saying, is you can break those rules. You can smash them up like

Schoenberg breaks the rules of composition and invents the twelve-tone scale and you get something that's atonal, and challenging, and difficult, but it's only *a*tonal *because* tonal exists. Schoenberg is breaking rules to create dissonance. There's nothing wrong with that (it can be incredibly invigorating), but it *has* to imply logically that *tonal* must exist. The very act of disruption proves the existence of the enemy. It confers legitimacy on its antagonist in the revolution. There is no greater confirmation of an archetype than in the work of Samuel Beckett, Albert Ayler or the Non-Dramatic Theatre movement. Ayler's free jazz destructions – remarkable in so many ways – confirm the existence of the melody. Sounding "wrong" is incredibly powerful but underlines there is a "right". So what is that "right"?

Aaron Sorkin, who I expect you'll be familiar with, said this: "The real rules are the rules of drama, the rules that Aristotle talks about. The fake TV rules are the ones that dumb TV execs will tell you: 'You can't do this; you've got to do that. You need three of these and five of those.' Those things are silly."

My favourite TV rule of all time was handed down some years ago by a commissioning editor, long since retired. He once declaimed, "You can never have a successful drama in which you see the sea." This governed a major broadcasting network's policy for ten years. During those ten years the network – and its drama – were insanely successful. They clobbered the opposition. He was hailed as a saviour. This was twenty or thirty years ago. But… the biggest hit in the *last* ten years on British television is *Broadchurch*, and of course he'd never have commissioned it. Rules – fake rules – can take you to funny places sometimes. What can you conclude? That twenty years ago audiences weren't ready for the sea? Or more probably that showing the sea is not a pre-requisite of success. There are rules and there is superstition. In drama it's easy to confuse the two.

But…

There are certain principles that govern drama and you cannot write properly until you understand both what they are and why they are there. It's not about obeying or disobeying rules. It's about mastering craft skills, so I'd like to talk a little about those.

"When forced to work within a strict framework, the imagination is taxed to its utmost and will produce the richest results. Given total freedom, the work is likely to sprawl."

It's T.S. Eliot, and I first discovered the truth of this when I began my career in television, storylining *EastEnders*. You stare at a blank piece of paper, not a single idea in your head. You're in terrible trouble, then someone says, "You've got to write Danny Dyer out because he's going on *I Want to Be a Celebrity* in three weeks time," you've suddenly got a restriction, and that restriction gives you a story. Rules help. Friedrich Engels said something that got to the heart of this: "Freedom is the recognition of necessity". Total freedom is meaningless. Form is important, structure is vital. Rules help. So the question thus becomes, as Sorkin suggested: what *are* those real rules?

I started writing *Into The Woods* for a number of reasons, but one of the main reasons it came about was because every screenwriting book never referenced other narrative forms.

I went to see Professor John Mullan at the University of London, because I wanted to talk to an academic about the rules of storytelling. I was convinced that if *Save The Cat* and *The Writer's Journey* were true, they had to be true for all narrative forms – novels, plays, documentary, even advertising. So I asked him, "What do you think of Robert McKee?" and he just looked at me and he said, "Who?" Professor Mullan is an expert in his field. He's an expert on narrative. He knows everything. He'd never heard of him.

I talked to him about the plethora of screenwriting books. He seemed fascinated, but had no knowledge of them nor the people who wrote them. Why? Because in academic circles nobody takes them seriously.

And of course the reason they aren't taken seriously is the reason I touched on at the beginning of this chapter. They are without empirical foundation. They are built on sand. *"Why?"* has to be central to everything. You can't just observe. You have to prove.

So. What are the real rules?

How do we perceive the world? A ridiculous question to ask, but here are two pictures: there's a cute looking baby, and there's a lighted match. In really simple terms: child touches match, it hurts, child learns never to touch match again.

That's how perception works: I see the world, I look at it, I draw conclusions. It's a fundamental, basic act we cannot avoid. We think dialectically. In simple terms, thought and perception works like that.

Thesis: I exist; antithesis: I perceive the outside world which is the opposite to myself; synthesis: I change, so I become different.

It's the fundamental process by which humans assimilate knowledge: find something new, explore it, and assimilate it. You sit here, you listen to me and you go away changed. Whether you agree with what I say or not you will draw conclusions. However subtly, the way you view the world will alter. Something new has been delivered to you which you can accept or dismiss – it doesn't matter which – and either way a dialectical has occurred, just as it occurs in every microsecond of every day, because in every microsecond we're ordering the world. We're turning the world into narrative, because a world without narrative is impossible to comprehend. We're turning the world into story.

We're imposing order on something that is fundamentally so big, so large, we cannot possibly imagine the scale and shape of it. Every time we come across alien phenomena, we explore it, we find its essential truth, and we assimilate it. We file it into a system. Now that could be "Matches hurt," or, if we have a clinical disorder, "Matches are fun". It works the same way: we observe, we assimilate, we change. I hear there's a lecture about the use and abuse of narrative structure, I go to it and listen intensely, I conclude it's rubbish/genius/somewhere in between. That's it. You cannot *not* do that. It's just a law of physics. It's a law of nature.

Let's look at a children's story.

Jack swaps beans for cow, beanstalk grows, Jack goes up beanstalk and steals golden egg, giant wakes up, chases Jack, Jack chops down beanstalk, giant is killed, Jack lives happily ever after.

What you see in *Jack and the Beanstalk* is the act of perception *dramatised*. *Thesis*: he exists, *antithesis*: he discovers a whole new world, *synthesis*: he assimilates the lessons of that new world: it changes him. All storytelling is fundamentally built on this pattern. This is the '*why*'– the act of perception dramatised.

So, three acts: thesis, antithesis, synthesis. Three acts – classic Hollywood structure. A character is flawed in the first act; they are thrown into a world opposite of everything they believe in or have ever understood in the second act; and in the last act they change, overcome their flaw and are healed. It sounds simplistic, but have a look at the last film you saw. In both *Son of Saul*, and *Captain America: Civil War* – you'll see the pattern there.

I'd like, if I may, to use the example of a number of Pixar films. Partly because a lot of people know them, partly because they're incredibly archetypal, but also because – if I may be subjective for a moment – they are the epitome of the storyteller's art. We start, as they did, with *Toy Story*. Its hero – a benevolent dictator Woody, who, on the arrival of his nemesis, is thrown out of his bedroom window, and finds himself in an entirely alien world. What does he do? He has to learn to cooperate with Buzz Lightyear, and only by doing that can they both get home and live happily ever after. There's a very similar pattern in *Finding Nemo*: the over-controlling Marlon (Tom Hanks) loses his child, child runs off, he chases after him, so he's thrown into a world completely opposite of everything he believes in. In the end of course Marlon finds and helps rescue Nemo, but learns a very important lesson – you can't be over-controlling, you have to let your children play. And finally *Cars*. Here a mad, arrogant racing driver wants to win the Piston Cup, finds himself completely abandoned in a strange town, the antithesis of every value he's ever believed in, and of course learns the values of that town. He learns to be kind and that winning isn't everything. He goes back to the race, which he could win, but he chooses not to, instead helping another injured car. Arrogance – opposite – benevolence; thesis – antithesis – synthesis. In *Toy Story*, in *Finding Nemo*, in *Cars*.

This pattern applies pretty much to every narrative you've ingested since you were born. A ridiculously sweeping statement, but have a look. A character is established, you confront them with their opposite, and you synthesise the two to achieve balance.

What's fascinating about this is that we do it without thinking. Have a look at something you wrote. Dig deep enough, and I'm fairly sure you will find that pattern somewhere there. Why does *Jack and the Beanstalk* have the same structure as any Pixar film or any arthouse film? Why does it have the same structure as something *you* wrote?

Because structure is a biological and physical process, not something plucked out of the air by Syd Field. It's the process of perception *dramatised* – and it forms the basic structural model not just of every feature film, but of all narrative. We can't not do it. We do it unconsciously. "Dramatic structure is not arbitrary", as David Mamet, who has written more sense about screenwriting than almost anybody said, "Drama is our way of ordering the universe into a comprehensible form".

There are few better examples of three-act structure than David Hare's adaptation of the Bernard Schlenk novel, *The Reader*. Like the book it is based on, it tells the story of a young boy in post-war Germany who falls in love with a much older woman. One day she completely disappears. That's act one. In act two he learns, exactly halfway through the film, that she was in fact a camp guard at Auschwitz, and so the person he thought she was is exactly the opposite of who he now knows she is. In the last act he learns why she did what she did and very slowly starts to no longer condemn but to try and understand – thesis, antithesis, synthesis; love, hate, understanding. Three acts, a classic hero's journey, the very thing David Hare is so wary of he cannot help but practise himself.

Pan's Labyrinth by Guillermo del Toro – a journey into the woods. The same journey Craig, the fictional protagonist of Charlie Kaufman's *Being John Malkovich*, undergoes – a man who can only find happiness by climbing into someone else's head. Hare, Kaufman, del Toro – they all do it. It doesn't diminish what they do, which is often brilliant, but… it has an incredibly unfortunate side-effect.

There's so much nonsense spouted, written, tweeted and taught about screenwriting that intelligent people, people like Hare and Kaufman and del Toro, understandably run away from "Put it there". They decry all study as rubbish. And it's not.

8

That for me is the biggest sadness. The plethora of nonsense talked about narrative structure actually belittles our ability to analyse what we do seriously. I think it's wrong that universities in our country don't teach the study of narrative. I think it's wrong that apart from AC Bradley – Professor of Poetry at Oxford at the beginning of the 20th century – I couldn't find anyone outside the Russian Formalists in the last hundred years who approached it with the intellectual application it deserved. It's sad, and it's sad because it leaves a vacuum that sucks the snake oil salesmen in.

That's the end of act two of this talk, by the way. It's time to come back home. And to the question with which we began – can you teach writing?

I've tried to argue that structure is almost certainly a projection of inner psychological conflict. I exist, I perceive an outside world that is overwhelming, I assimilate it in a way that I can tame, I feel safe, I move on. Arguably therefore the process is instinctive, to which I would say, well yes, up to a point, because everybody writes in a different way. I work with loads of writers. Half of them write completely instinctively and say, "I do not want to know about structure. I have no interest in it at all."

There's one with whom I'm working with at the moment: "I hear you've written a book," he said, "I'm not going to read it. I suspect it's jolly good, but it will probably make me worse." It's absolutely fair. It might make him worse, because he believes – and it works, because he writes beautifully – that it comes totally from within.

Others write completely methodically and spend a month writing a scene-by-scene breakdown, and only when that structure is perfect do they, in a blaze of glory, write the dialogue in an hour and then send it in. That's how they do it – and of course many of them write just as beautifully as the others as well.

From that surely there can only be one conclusion – successful writers understand structure whether they know it or not. Jimmy McGovern, Peter Moffat or Tony Jordan – the shining lights of our industry – may decry structure, yet arguably they're the best proponents of dramatic structure of all. Isn't that extraordinary that they do it – not because they study it, but because it echoes a call from within?

Another conclusion we can perhaps extrapolate from this is, and forgive me for going back to the beginning again, writing is a craft. The more you write, the more you discover that echo within yourself. Arguably, it takes years of effort, years of practice, years of rejection before you achieve mastery of that craft. Just like playing football, just like playing an instrument to professional level, you're not going to be good straight away.

Many new writers are oblivious to the rules of writing or wilfully choose to ignore them. That's fine, but, unconsciously or not, every time you write you learn the rules of structure, because every time you write you go, "Does that work? I don't think that works. I'll do that." What you're finding is that you're chiselling away at the marble within which perfect structure is encased, waiting to be uncovered. How do you uncover it? Through years of practice, years of frustration, years of toil. But most importantly perhaps – years of learning to understand that it *is* a skill, it *is* a craft.

The art critic Robert Hughes got annoyed about many things, but there was one subject he returned to continually – a belief that became prevalent in America in the 1970s that formal training wasn't required. "Just paint. Just let it all out", he felt was one of the great curses of modern art.

Furious at the abandoning of line-drawing in art schools he declared in *The Shock of the New:*

"With scarcely an exception, every significant artist of the last hundred years, from Seurat to Matisse, from Picasso to Mondriaan, from Beckmann to de Kooning, was drilled, or drilled themselves, in academic drawing – the long tussle with the unforgiving and real motif which, in the end, proved to be the only basis on which the real formal achievements of Modernism could be raised… The philosophical beauty of Mondriaan's squares and grids begins with the empirical beauty of his apple trees." They learnt ruthlessly and rigorously to draw and that's what made them great.

That is I believe, in the end, the answer. You can teach writing – but you can't teach genius. However, genius doesn't exist without some kind of understanding – conscious or not – of knowledge of their craft. What you can do, then, is allow people the space to play, and provide them with the knowledge to experiment with themselves and create. Give them the tools and the best will finish the job. Cézanne, Picasso, Kandinsky, Miro, de Kooning and Matisse all grew up in the atelier system, learning from the masters of line drawing, before they embarked on modernism – and transformed the world within which they worked. They were ruthlessly schooled in the basics of their craft.

Caveat, obviously: "By logic and reason we die hourly; by imagination we live." You can write the greatest structure in the world and still be a terrible writer. Students often used to say to me, "Where do I put the Inciting Incident?" I'd say, "Don't worry. Just do it. You'll find it. It will find you". Understanding rules will only produce dead writing if not coupled with the inspiration that must run alongside.

So what I say to my students now is, "Study. Write all the time. Learn structure in the hope that you will forget it. Think of it like riding a bike. Practise enough to do it unconsciously".

I've been very lucky. In the ten years I've been teaching narrative I've been able to watch that process first hand. When I first set up the BBC Writers Academy some pretty good writers came and joined the course… and immediately got worse. But then, slowly they got better, and every year they improved some more, and of those writers now, four have their own series on British television, an extraordinary achievement in itself, but in addition 85% have maintained a career in the industry. They did it partly because we were lucky in our selection, but also because they killed themselves to understand, and then killed themselves again practising their craft.

So in the end the most important thing to remember when learning to be a writer is not 'how to'. What's important is 'why?' The question you ask when you ask what you're doing is not "I must follow this pattern", it's "Why am I writing this here?". You're a carpenter, marrying craft and inspiration. If you understand that everything else falls into place.

One last quote. Delacroix.

"First, learn to be a craftsman. It won't keep you from being a genius."

8

INTERVIEW NINE
STEPHEN JEFFREYS

BY ANNIE HERRIDGE

ANNIE HERRIDGE: I'm going to go through what Stephen Jeffreys has done. Stephen wrote the play *The Libertine*, and he also wrote the film of the same name with Johnny Depp playing the lead role. He has also written *I Just Stopped by to See the Man* for the Royal Court Theatre, *Valued Friends* for Hampstead Theatre and *Bugles at the Gates of Jalalabad*, part of *The Great Game*, a series of plays about Afghanistan for the Tricycle Theatre. He was also Literary Associate at the Royal Court and he is on the Board of the Royal Court. He is a writing tutor at RADA and he does the Masterclasses there, and now he is one of our Masters. He has done a lot.

Stephen, as a playwright, can you tell us more about who you are?

STEPHEN JEFFREYS: My family for 150 years made billiard tables, so we've always been in the entertainment business – there's been some continuity there. I think I'm the first person in our family to go into the theatre.

ANNIE HERRIDGE: How did your mum and dad feel about that?

STEPHEN JEFFREYS: They were very pleased. They both liked going to the theatre. My mum was very interested in words and they encouraged me a lot.

ANNIE HERRIDGE: Coming from a working-class background or from a background of trade, how did you feel going into the theatre? Did you feel intimidated?

STEPHEN JEFFREYS: I did. It took me a long time to realise that you could actually break through into that world. I think it's easier now. I think that people are more comfortable with switching classes. We always spoke very nicely, but we were common as muck really, and so it was a quite interesting world to go into. I felt nervous when I first was with actors, and then that changed.

I was talking with John Godber the other day. I've known John for years, and someone very important in my life, Clive Wolfe, who ran the National Student Drama Festival for years and years and years, died the other day, and I organised his funeral and John was there.

We were talking quite a lot about this subject, because John came from a mining background in South Yorkshire and there was no theatre in his family at all. We all have different backgrounds but there was some kind of rapport there.

I think this country is less dominated by class than it was. I think it's unfortunately more dominated by money than it was, but I think there's a little bit of fluidity in background.

When I first went into theatre, I thought it was a little bit of a closed door, but that's changed.

ANNIE HERRIDGE: My second question is can you tell us about what you do in terms of teaching dramatic writing?

STEPHEN JEFFREYS: I've always tried to teach a craft. I never tell people what they should write. The first time I went to a writing workshop I was running it and that meant that I had no background in that and I just began to teach things that I discovered.

I think when you start writing you just follow your nose. You follow your instincts and gradually you find that you need aspects of craft. Quite a lot of writers are able to write their first two or three plays with a certain amount of freedom and on an impulse.

As you go deeper and deeper into it, I think you find you need to know more about the craft. For me, knowing more about craft evolved because I had been a teacher, and it evolved via teaching craft. As soon as I found something out that I needed to know, I realised there was probably a way of communicating it to other people. Generally speaking I've worked in that way in my teaching over the years.

I found, after a while, that there were certain areas that I didn't stray into. I didn't teach classes about character, for instance. Then I decided, "Well, let me find out about that". Really I was working on two different fronts – I was working as a playwright, but also slightly as an academic and thinking, "How would I approach character from almost an academic point of view?" as well as how I actually did it myself.

Over the years, I've built up a repertoire of different workshops which I do and that's what I teach. The main point of teaching is to give people their own voice – to say, "What we are interested in is your own voice and how you articulate that, and what I can give you is certain tools which will get you there quicker".

I wasted years and years of my playwriting life because I didn't know what I was doing and I try to say to people, "Do this and this and it will save you time".

I think when I started, certainly up until the mid-eighties, the playwriting culture in this country was extremely amateurish. There was a resistance – you kind of thought, "Well, writers are these romantic individuals who have these fantastic ideas and somehow they are being encumbered by ideas about structure and craft".

That's changed a lot. I think Robert McKee, who was a much maligned character, did a great deal to change that – he brought a lot of the screenwriting concepts to a lot of people in theatre. We assimilated those and we began to think much more professionally.

I think that young writers now in their early twenties know a great deal more, for instance, than I did when I was in my early twenties.

ANNIE HERRIDGE: When we were learning theatre writing, there was a question that kept coming up though for all the writers – "plot or character?" May I ask you that question?

STEPHEN JEFFREYS: That was the question that interested Aristotle and he came down on the side of plot. However, I think in a way that they are two sides of the same coin – plot is simply character in action.

The character doesn't exist without plot – in a novel, the character could almost exist on its own, you can describe characters, but in plays it's what a character does. People can say something about a character or a character can say something about themselves, but it's what they do which takes you through to the end.

In the end Hamlet becomes a killer, though he is not naturally a killer, and Elizabeth Proctor becomes a liar, although she is not naturally a liar, because that's what they do under the pressure of the plot, so the two things are two sides of the same coin.

ANNIE HERRIDGE: Now my third question: why do you do what you do?

STEPHEN JEFFREYS: I believe in new plays and I've spent quite a lot of time passing on what I know to other writers because you want a very vivid and vigorous theatre culture. I've been lucky to meet writers like Abi Morgan, Simon Stephens and Roy Williams early in their careers and maybe influenced them.

I think as a result of not just of what I've done, but a general professionalisation of their writing culture, people know much more about the technical side of writing. That doesn't mean they are going to write good plays, because writing good plays is always about what's within and what the writer wants to say, but at least they don't waste a lot of time writing the wrong kind of play or writing within the wrong kind of structure.

ANNIE HERRIDGE: Do you think that structure is important then too?

STEPHEN JEFFREYS: It's something I've done because it seemed to be something that people were afraid of.

I was asked about ten years ago to work with a group of writers at the Royal Court to do some sessions with them and everybody said, "Tell me about structure, I'm terrified of it".

There are certain principles of dramatic structure. However, the point about it is for people to find their own structures, to find how they want to write, how to find your voice within the principles of dramatic writing. Things like finding the climactic moments and finding the gaps between the climactic moments. Working with different textures – that's something that you can teach people to be aware of, but they must make it their own.

I've never been a prescriptive teacher. I suppose what I teach is, "Here are some techniques you can use, but they are there to be used so that you can inhabit them with your own words and you can take control".

I do a whole session on experimental structures, for instance, and most of those experimental structures arise out of an understanding of traditional structure. There's a certain similarity to those cubist painters – Picasso didn't suddenly start painting cubist paintings, he had other phases he'd gone through to get to that.

To understand how you might experiment, one of the best ways of doing it is to work out how do traditional structures work, how do I subvert them, and how do I work with them?

ANNIE HERRIDGE: So you need to know craft to be able to break the mould or break the rules?

STEPHEN JEFFREYS: Yes. Caryl Churchill is someone who has a very strong understanding of traditional structures. For instance, *Top Girls* is a classic and is a take-off of a three-act play – it's actually a classic three-act play which has been somehow undermined. Her approach was to do that – to take the three-act play and do something different with it.

I think people have said this throughout the Masterclasses – know your own voice, that's what counts. I spent eleven years reading five plays a week at the Royal Court and in the end you know on page two whether someone has their own voice or not and once you are aware of their own voice you think, "Oh yes, this is something I haven't done before" and that's what you want.

We had this thing at the Royal Court where after *The Weir* we had all these plays set in pubs.

After *Mojo* there were all these plays where a dismembered head or some other body part would appear.

There was a whole silliness of, "Well you had done this before so let's do it again". No, that's not what theatres want – theatres want your own voice, something new.

ANNIE HERRIDGE: What else do you believe writers need to know about dramatic writing?

STEPHEN JEFFREYS: I've spent quite a long time pushing certain ideas about – not only just about story structure, but also about the way that people use structure.

To be simple about this, structure is a combination of three elements: time, space and story. How do you use time, space and story? Those are the ingredients. A play which is set in one room in continuous time over the space of an hour and a half, like Conor McPherson's *The Weir*, is inherently different from a play like David Hare and Howard Brenton's *Pravda* which is a multi-scene set in many locations.

One of my main interests has been trying to get people to use the right structure because certain structures are right for certain plays.

There is no point in using an experimental structure if your play is on a new subject and a real *zeitgeist* play which is new to you and new to the audience. You just do it in the simplest way possible because you're onto something new.

However, if you are doing a very well worn theme, then you might need to find some different way of doing it – the way that you combine time, space and story is infinitely variable.

I think a lot of writers don't understand that importance. People get into a riff of following rather laboriously these rather obvious film structures. What they need to do is to think about, "How do I make this slightly different, how do I work this my way?" and giving people the insight into the elements of structure helps. I'm not a great one for experiment for its own sake but it's finding the right structure for what you want to say.

I think the idea behind that is it's going to carry the play. It's not some academic notion that you place on top, it's the overall shape that will give you imaginative ideas.

When working with structure, people think of it sometimes with a certain amount of fear and they worry about, "Am I doing it the way Aristotle said?" That's not the point, the point is, "Does it express what you want to say?" One of the things that I teach is how you use different dramatic shapes for different dramatic effects.

ANNIE HERRIDGE: One final question: if you could tell writers one thing what would it be?

STEPHEN JEFFREYS: I would say that you have to be good at being on your own. The thing that people think and get obsessed by is, "Oh well, being a writer is great, you are in rehearsal or you are doing interviews." In fact the reality is that you spend most of every day on your own. That's the reality and people say, "Oh, I've got this great idea for a play, I've started it" and then you see them again a couple of years later and they still haven't got anywhere with it.

The point is they don't actually like being on their own or they are unable to be on their own. If you are a writer, you have to be someone who can be on your own. You can sit in a room for eight hours and at the end of it you will have done something. That's not an easy skill and not everybody can do it. I would say if you can train yourself to do it for an hour then that's a good start. However, nowadays everyone is on their mobile or being enticed out by drinking. Someone once said, in the seventies I think, "That the greatest enemy to the writer is the telephone" because someone phones up and says, "Do you fancy coming out for a drink now?" My ideal – the studio I write in now – has no internet connection.

ANNIE HERRIDGE: Stephen, I'm going to hand over to you for your Masterclass.

MASTERCLASS NINE
PLAYWRITING

BY STEPHEN JEFFREYS

When I first started writing I had a huge stroke of luck as I wrote a play for the National Student Drama Festival.

Michael Codron, the producer, had been in the habit of giving a reasonable cash prize for the best play at the National Student Drama Festival. The year I won it he had stopped giving the meaningful cash prize. However, Clive Wolfe, who ran the National Student Drama Festival and was a very influential figure, sent the play to him and said, "This would have been the play you would have given the award to".

Very kindly, Michael invited me to his office in Regent Street to talk about things and he said, "You really need an agent". I said, "I don't know how to get an agent". "Well," he said, "the best agent is Peggy Ramsay" – you may have seen Peggy Ramsay played by Vanessa Redgrave in the film about Joe Orton, and it was a very accurate portrayal. Michael Codron said, "Why don't you just walk there now, it's only a ten-minute walk?"

This story has a point to it.

I wandered across to just off St Martin's Lane. There's a tiny alleyway called Goodwin's Court and it was there Peggy had her life really, which was talking to writers.

I was ushered up into the room outside where her room was. She was closeted with an American director called Alan Schneider who was the director of Samuel Beckett in America – he was Beckett's man in America.

After about ten minutes, Peggy, who was a very voluble woman who was then in her, I suppose, early seventies, came out with Alan Schneider. She said, "Ah Stephen, Alan is off to Paris this weekend to see Sam. Alan, make sure you give Sam Stephen's best wishes" and I thought how great for Sam Beckett to get the regards of this completely unknown writer.

I was then ushered into her presence and she talked at me for about an hour and eventually I said to her, "Well, what advice would you give to a young writer?"

She said, "Are you right-handed?"

This made no sense to me but I said, "Yes".

She said, "You must find something to do with your left hand".

I was still baffled and I said, "What do you mean?"

She said, "I wasn't brought up in this country, I was brought up in Africa, so that when I came here and played all these house tennis parties in the 1920s and 30s, I was much better at tennis than everybody else" and I still couldn't see where we were getting to.

Then she said, "So in the end I had to play with my left hand to give them all a chance. And when I played with my left hand, all day playing tennis with my left hand, I had the most wonderful dreams".

I began to see where we were going.

She said, "What happened was that the use of the left hand stimulated the right side of the brain and that stimulated the subconscious. It's important that writers stimulate their subconscious".

That was a rather strange introduction of an idea to me – and I think that our knowledge of the left and right side of the brain has changed slightly – but it certainly is true that you can identify writers as being generally either left-brain or right-brain types.

The left-brain types do the organisation well – they organise the characters coming off stage, the climaxes, the climatic moments of where they should be, the interval is where it should be – but the plays are often not particularly full of heart and not particularly believable.

Whereas the other type, the ones who have been playing tennis with their left hand all day, the right-brain writers, tend to have a great strength in characterisation, metaphor, making pictures on the stage, delving into the subconscious, all of which is fascinating, but quite often the plays that they write are un-performable because they are just a mass of wonderful ideas which don't add up to anything.

When I started work at the Royal Court Theatre in the early 1990s, reading a lot of plays, you could make three piles of plays – the pile of plays which were competent but dull, the pile of plays which were fascinating but un-performable, and the group in the middle which were potential plays that you could put on.

I think from that hint from Peggy, and from the subsequent work of reading a lot of plays, I began to be aware that playwrights are often either left-brain or right-brain. They either do the organisational side of playwriting very well or they do the metaphoric side of playwriting very well. I think whenever I've done workshops with groups, you often find that people instinctively identify with one type or the other.

What I've tried to do with my writing workshops is always to say, "Work on what you're not good at". There are certain things that come easy to us all as writers – whether it's writing dialogue or character or plot. Certain things come easy and certain things are not easy. The point is to work on the things that are difficult for you and what is not immediately within your grasp. That's what we have to address. It's a slightly crude breakdown, but it seems to me to hold true.

The odd thing about playwriting which sets it apart from other kinds of writing, is that you're working with two different sets of skills at the same time. You are working simultaneously on something which is organised, which a stage manager can run, and which will unfold as a narrative, but you're also working on something which is a complex metaphor – the great plays always become metaphors.

The Cherry Orchard is a play about people who spend most of their time not worrying about what's happened to the cherry orchard. The cherry orchard means different things to different people and in the end you can't reduce what the cherry orchard means because it becomes a metaphor. On one level it's a simple play about economics. It's a play about, "We can't run this house, so we are going to have to sell it, so who is going to buy it?" That's one level of it. The other level is "What does the cherry orchard mean?" This level is connected with childhood, memory, the subconscious and character.

What I put forward to you as my basic thesis about writing for the theatre is that it's both of those things.

It's a highly visual medium – I think it's about 50% visual. When you ask people to describe, "What is the greatest moment of a play they have seen?" they never remember a line of dialogue. What they remember is a picture, so what you have to do is make pictures on the stage.

However, at the same time, it has to be intellectually coherent. Nearly always the theatre play tells a story and it has a subject. It sums up, in the way that Ola was saying earlier on, something which is a thesis for the play.

However, plays are complex. The reason why we write plays rather than the mottos in Christmas crackers is that they are complex, so the thesis of our play, although it's very important, is never all of the play – the ideas within the play become complex through the action of the characters in the plot.

I'd like to give you a couple of examples from The Year of Experimentation Festival of one of my methods I teach to bring this out.

The examples are all people who were writing a play. I asked them to describe the play they were writing and to use in a single sentence the word "but". So, if they were to describe *The Cherry Orchard*, they might say, "The three sisters want to go to Moscow, but they can't do that unless their brother, Andre, has a successful career as a professor". That's an economic idea which is something that underlines the three sisters.

Here are the examples:

JULIE: She has finally met a man who shows a genuine care and love for her, but she is not even a human being. A diabolical ghost embodied in a young woman instead."

The point about this exercise is that beforehand you show what is 'the desire' that moves the play – so we have this woman who is, in fact, we find out, a ghost and she has found the perfect man at last.

Then after the "but", we have what is the problem and what is the obstacle as plays move forward by conflict. She has finally found the perfect man, but the problem is that she is a ghost.

You can see straightaway this is a play – there is some amazing conflict. Where is it going to go from there? We understand from looking at that sentence that there is going to be a resolution of the conflict. Within that sentence is not only what the play is about, but also its structure.

How Julie writes this is up to her, but it's quite possible that one could start with a meeting together of these two people who seem to get on very well. However, one of them is not actually a human being so that creates problems.

It also begs the question, "What is the resolution?" What is the resolution in this conflict? How do we get to the end of this? Via that question, there is something which should fascinate the audience and should be surprising and rather intriguing.

What we are looking at here is a rather interesting combination of left-brain and right-brain thinking. On one level this is a love story, and one of the hardest things to write are love stories as they have been done so many times before, so you have to find a new way in. On another level we are moving away from the realism of it – we are moving into a psychologically complex area. I think that audiences are always intrigued by that. So there is a level on which it's a love story and a realistic story, and a level on which it's a ghost story.

Here is another example:

AUDIENCE MEMBER: Jeremy wants to move away from the city and break up with the dull routine of his repressed suburban life, but the guilt that he feels for his stubborn grieving mother is holding him back.

This is a play about a man whose aspiration is to get away, but he is held back by something, in this case by the guilt of his grieving mother. Why is she grieving?

Again you can see the shape of the play building up, you can see the character wanting something, but there is an obstacle and that is the essence of the drama.

Somehow that's resolved – you can't imagine this being resolved in some supernatural way but you can imagine it being resolved in terms of a real personal struggle.

In some ways you could say quite a lot of plays are about people trying to break out and what it is that holds them back and that makes a very intriguing piece.

There's a wonderful play by Marsha Norman called *Night Mother* in which a woman comes out at the start of the play and tells her mother that she is going to commit suicide. Within the playing out of the play we are going to see whether that happens or not, so it may be interesting to try and put a time frame on it.

These are people who are locked into a relationship and the working out of the logic of the play is to break out of that, to break out into a new world, or an attempt to break out. Whether or not they are successful depends on the writer, but there are two different ways of getting there – either he breaks out of that world or he is drawn back into it.

Here's another example:

AUDIENCE MEMBER: I've got an old man who is attacked by a young girl in his video shop. It's a seemingly mindless attack, but the man doesn't remember that he was involved in destroying her life.

This is quite a complicated one because we have some back story straight away here and it becomes intriguing. What appears to be a mindless, motiveless attack actually has a psychological reality because this guy has done something terrible to her. This is a play which is in some way going to go back and delve into the past.

To a large extent, the exercise which we are describing here, where you have to describe in a sentence the play, is quite hard work for a lot of writers. You think, "Oh it's much more complicated than that". Well, yes it is much more complicated than that, but by simplifying and by saying, "Let's reduce the play to a single sentence, a desire and an obstacle", that quite often frees you.

Something you can do with this exercise, as writers, is when you are working on a play just to write in a single sentence what it is – write it down and carry on working on the play. Two or three weeks later you may have a slightly different sentence. If you do that then there's a sense that that's a clue that you are getting somewhere, because quite often what you are articulating about the play changes. It becomes more complex. This is one of those paradoxical exercises where by simplifying something and by saying, "Okay, let's bore down to its basics," it actually lets you into a degree of more complexity.

I think there's a difference between plays that are complicated, which is you can't quite work out what they are about, and plays which are complex, which is they are not simple. *The Doll's House* is not simple – Nora's character is not completely good and her husband is not completely bad, but there's a basic line going through the play which is strong.

Trying to find that strong line through a play feels sometimes like a reductive exercise. In fact what it does is it clarifies things and then, as a result of that, things often become more complex.

Let's have one more example:

AUDIENCE MEMBER: Anna wants to help refugees of a flood, but they do not want the help she offers them.

This play is interesting straight away because we want to know more, and there's possible visual images there because we want to know about the psychological reality.

Then the idea of the active person of the play having her help rejected is extremely dramatic. The question is, "What happens then? What happens in the third act?"

You could say that the first act of the play, or the first part of this story, is Anna becoming interested in these people and in doing something for them. And there is some limited thing that she does for them – that's the end of act one.

Act two is this growing revulsion towards Anna – why these people do not want to be helped and then that begs the question of "What happens in act three?" This is what we all want to know about. How does this thing wind up?

This is, of course, the classic – the reason why stories remain very popular in the theatre. The theatre happens in front of our eyes, in real time and space, and we want to follow the story. Traditional story-telling is probably most alive in the theatre in a similar way to how, in the novel, one has quite a lot of different ways of telling stories.

Quite traditional plays will continue to be written with relatively traditional story-telling because it unfolds before our very eyes and we want to know what the hell happens next.

With this play the intrigue is what's going to happen in the third act – we see this good woman who has a noble impulse, the impulse is rejected. How is it resolved?

That's the thing you've got to write.

CONCLUSION

BY JENNIFER TUCKETT

I hope you have enjoyed and found useful *Dramatic Writing Masterclasses: Key Advice from the Industry Masters*. My own chapter is more of a summary than a Masterclass, but I hope will shed some useful light on why I hope it is helpful to bring industry and university training together to explore the future of dramatic writing training in the UK.

The first MA in Creative Writing was created in 1970 by Malcolm Bradbury and Angus Wilson at the University of East Anglia and the first MA in Playwriting was created in 1989 by David Edgar at Birmingham University. Since then, there has been an expansion of creative writing degrees, often focused on a model of the writers' workshop, providing writers with feedback on their work.

My feeling is that the next stage should provide greater access to and insight into the industry as part of training the next generation of writers.

Why would you want to do this and does it affect the idea of an artist? I don't think so. A doctor trains at a hospital, in addition to a university. A teacher trains at a school in addition to a university. A traditional Master Craftsman would complete an apprenticeship in the industry prior to becoming a journeyman, using his new-found knowledge to create a portfolio of Masterpieces, after which he would become a Master. It seems to me logical but also important that, when so many excellent apprenticeship programmes have emerged in recent years, teaching should now work together with the industry to provide improved access to how it works.

As an example of why I believe this is important and effective: prior to joining Central Saint Martins, I worked at a university which didn't teach playwriting training in their creative writing department – when I joined the department, I was told there was no interest. In the first year of the industry-partnered playwriting module I set up, eight students registered to take the course, of whom two secured placements at the Royal Exchange Theatre. In the second year, forty signed up, several secured places on professional writing attachment programmes and one undergraduate beat off undergraduate and postgraduate competition to become one of seven finalists for the BBC Future Talent Award. In the third year, eighty students signed up, of which six were produced by the BBC. In the fourth year, I set up for that university the UK's first formally industry partnered MA in

Playwriting, training the next generation of writers in the region in which it is based, with 50% of the course taught by three of the region's leading theatres.

I believe that industry partnerships changed the culture of that university into one in which students can and have begun to successfully work and earn money from their writing.

The increase in student numbers and success was from having access to the right industry training, to understanding who worked in those jobs, to seeing that these are people like us, to thinking about and knowing how these jobs worked, what they were looking for, how the development process works, what was being taught on training programmes, what criteria scripts are being assessed by, and what the industry is.

That university also recruited students from the most deprived 1% of the country, another reason why I believe access to training is important: you shouldn't have to live in London, and/or be able to attend workshops, to know how the industry works and who's training writers and what they think. That's why we're providing access for the first time to what has hitherto largely been unpublished training advice. For example Masters like Kate Rowland, Philip Shelley, Ola Animashawun, Fin Kennedy and Steve Winter have never published their training advice and methods before this book.

At Central Saint Martins, we're expanding this work to cover all forms of dramatic writing training, as we think a career in this field increasingly moves between forms. I hope this book can be used for various purposes, from providing key advice, inspiration and an insight into who is working in these industry roles for writers, to assisting teachers in schools and universities, and to provide an insight into the different models of training and current thought around dramatic writing training.

At its best, I believe dramatic writing training should train us in what we need to know as writers for a long and sustainable career – I hope this benefits the writers, the industry and the audience members who see our work.

This is the first in a series; future books will provide in-depth access to each form of industry training – from writing for the theatre to film, radio, television and digital media. The next in the series is *The Student Guide to Writing: Playwriting* which takes you step-by-step through the process of writing a play, with playwriting lesson plans by those leading the way in industry training.

I want to conclude by saying thank you to all of our Masters, to the MA Dramatic Writing students who helped create the In Conversation chapters and finally to you for taking part in the culmination of our Year of Experimentation via this book.

Here's to the future of dramatic writing training and, in our writer training, to attaining the key advice and the right skill-set needed in order to express the ideas and the stories that we want to tell in the best possible way, and in order to have successful and sustainable careers as writers.

10

BIOGRAPHIES

OLA ANIMASHAWUN: Ola Animashawun founded the Royal Court Theatre's Young Writers Programme, one of the world's most influential training programmes for young writers. He is Associate Director at the Royal Court Theatre and Creative Director of Euphoric Ink.

KRITIKA ARYA: Kritika Arya was an MA Dramatic Writing student at Drama Centre London at Central Saint Martins and has worked with theatre companies including Tara Arts and with the Kevin Spacey Foundation.

TUYEN DO: Tuyen Do was an MA Dramatic Writing student at Drama Centre London at Central Saint Martins, has been Associate Artist at Tamasha Theatre Company and performed professionally including in the television series *24*.

ANNIE HERRIDGE: Annie Herridge was an MA Dramatic Writing student at Drama Centre London at Central Saint Martins and has worked in theatre as a writer and director.

DAN HORRIGAN: Dan Horrigan was an MA Dramatic Writing student at Drama Centre at Central Saint Martins and has been shortlisted for the King's Cross New Writing Award. He has had his work staged at Theatre503 and the Soho Theatre amongst other places.

STEPHEN JEFFREYS: Stephen Jeffreys was Literary Associate at the Royal Court Theatre for eleven years and is the creator of Masterclasses which have led the way in Playwriting teaching in the UK.

CAROLINE JESTER: Caroline Jester has been Dramaturg at Birmingham Repertory Theatre and is a Fellow of the Institute of Creative and Critical Writing at Birmingham City University. She is co writing and editing a book for Methuen Drama on Playwrights and their Craft in the UK and US and is co author of *Playwriting Across the Curriculum* (Routledge). She has pioneered collaborative and digital playwriting programmes worldwide.

PHILIP JONES: Philip Jones was an MA Dramatic Writing student at Drama Centre London at Central Saint Martins. He has twenty years experience as a documentary maker in television working on programmes including *Come Dine With Me, Geordie Shore* and *Rock n Roll Hotel*. As a writer, he won *The Guardian* short film award.

FIN KENNEDY: Fin Kennedy is the winner of the first Fringe First ever awarded for a schools production and Artistic Director of Tamasha Theatre Company.

LIBERTY MARTIN: Liberty Martin was an MA Dramatic Writing student at Drama Centre London at Central Saint Martins and has written and performed work at the Edinburgh Fringe Festival, Latitude Festival and also in London. Her short film was a winner of a BBC Writersroom scheme and an animated short film she helped write is currently in festivals around the world.

CHARLOTTE O'LEARY: Charlotte O'Leary was an MA Dramatic Writing student at Drama Centre London at Central Saint Martins and has worked for the BBC, was the producer of Fin Kennedy's first In Battalions Festival and recently had a play produced at the Old Operating Theatre.

KATE ROWLAND: Kate Rowland is the founder of BBC Writersroom, the BBC's new writing department, and has been the Creative Director of New Writing at the BBC, the Commissioner of Radio 3's The Wire strand, and the Head of BBC Radio Drama.

PHILIP SHELLEY: Philip Shelley runs the Channel 4 screenwriting course, one of the UK's leading screenwriting training programmes, and is also a script consultant, script editor and producer.

NINA STEIGER: Nina Steiger is Associate Director at the Soho Theatre, has been a Clore Fellow and has led the way in teaching writing for digital media as well as playwriting.

JENNIFER TUCKETT: Jennifer Tuckett is the first Course Leader for Drama Centre London at Central Saint Martin's new MA Dramatic Writing and previously founded the UK's first formally industry partnered MA in Playwriting, ran industry partnered pilot projects on training writers for radio drama and digital media with the BBC, and is the Director of Writers at Work Productions, which supports writers and new ways of working with writers in the industry.

STEVE WINTER: Steve Winter is Director of the Kevin Spacey Foundation and co-creator of the Old Vic New Voices 24 Hour Plays and TS Eliot US/UK Exchange.

JOHN YORKE: John Yorke is the creator of the BBC Writers Academy and has been the Managing Director of Company Pictures, Head of Channel 4 Drama and Controller of BBC Drama Production.

JULIE ZHENG: Julie Zheng was an MA Dramatic Writing student at Drama Centre London at Central Saint Martins and is a writer from China. She is currently developing an opera and worked at the Tete-a-Tete Opera Festival and has been selected for the Soho Theatre's Young Company.

10

First published in 2017 by Oberon Books Ltd
521 Caledonian Road, London N7 9RH
Tel: +44 (0) 20 7607 3637 / Fax: +44 (0) 20 7607 3629
e-mail: info@oberonbooks.com
www.oberonbooks.com

Editorial Copyright © Jennifer Tuckett, 2017

Individual contributions copyright © the authors, 2017

Jennifer Tuckett is hereby identified as editor of this work in accordance with section 77 of the Copyright, Designs and Patents Act 1988. The editor has asserted her moral rights.

You may not copy, store, distribute, transmit, reproduce or otherwise make available this publication (or any part of it) in any form, or binding or by any means (print, electronic, digital, optical, mechanical, photocopying, recording or otherwise), without the prior written permission of the publisher. Any person who does any unauthorized act in relation to this publication may be liable to criminal prosecution and civil claims for damages.

A catalogue record for this book is available from the British Library.

PB ISBN: 9781783193240
E ISBN: 9781783193257

Printed, bound and converted
by CPI Group (UK) Ltd, Croydon, CR0 4YY.

Visit www.oberonbooks.com to read more about all our books and to buy them. You will also find features, author interviews and news of any author events, and you can sign up for e-newsletters so that you're always first to hear about our new releases.